When you forget who you are, why you are, and where you are going, these are words that fall as gently and right as blossoms, a trail of grace through what you never expected. Lisa-Jo Baker's perfect pages will have you laughing and finding your rhythm again, have you hearing it again when you almost gave up—there—Him singing unconditional love over you. This is a book that is straight-from-the-hip honest, straight-out hilarious, and straight-from-God holy. Breathtaking. Life giving. Pure page-turning relief—pages I didn't want to end—that I will turn to again and again.

ANN VOSKAMP
Author of the *New York Times* bestsellers *One Thousand Gifts: A Dare to Live Fully Right Where You Are* and *The Greatest Gift: Unwrapping the Full Love Story of Christmas*

I so appreciate Lisa-Jo's gut-honest confessions as a woman who never dreamed of having children but who has now found God's healing love in motherhood. Lisa-Jo inspires me to look for God in every moment of my own beautiful but imperfect motherhood journey.

LYSA TERKEURST
New York Times bestselling author and president of Proverbs 31 Ministries

I don't know a woman who has taken on the enormous, daunting responsibility of raising a human being who says that it's exactly what she thought it would be. Because here's the thing: we'd all know she was lying. Motherhood is one of the great surprises of life, and Lisa-Jo has captured the essence of that with her exquisite words. Her fabulous voice lights up every page and makes you feel like you're sitting across from a dear friend as she tells her story and you see your own heart embedded within her words. As you turn the pages of this

book, you're in for a journey that will leave you nodding your head, smiling to yourself, and wishing you lived next door.

MELANIE SHANKLE
New York Times bestselling author of *Sparkly Green Earrings: Catching the Light at Every Turn*

Lisa-Jo has the undeniable gift of writing words that ache with pain but are always buoyed with the hope of redemption. I struggled alongside her in her grief, her doubts, and her fierce desire to be nothing less than who she was meant to be. And I rejoiced with her as she saw glimpses of the way the Lord guided her path and prepared her for each coming season. I saw in Lisa-Jo what I often see in myself without knowing how to express it—the weight of life's reality kissing what is yet to come. She is the young girl trying to learn to cook with her head over a stove as she stirs where her mother used to be. She is the bright student with a world waiting to be conquered. And she is the wife who never wanted children of her own. She is, at once, the one who doesn't know enough yet knows too much. And truly it is the same for all of us. To walk through the days with her, seeing the Lord's hand even when she didn't, is a powerful reminder of His tenderness toward us. This book is a gorgeous example of what happens when we choose to look into our most trying times with a longing for the truth that belies our own intuition and ultimately rests in the security of Christ alone. She is that girl—and I'm so grateful she is. Allow these pages to sink into your own story, blessing you with a lot of laughs, a deep sense of camaraderie, and above all else, a wild sense of hope.

ANGIE SMITH
Women of Faith speaker and bestselling author of *What Women Fear: Walking in Faith That Transforms* and *Chasing God*

I was surprised by *Surprised by Motherhood*—not because
I didn't already know that Lisa-Jo is a brilliant storyteller and
writer, but because I thought I was done with books about
motherhood. They so often just say the same thing and leave
me feeling tired. Lisa-Jo has a gift of revealing the sacred
beauty in the everydayness of mothering, and I found myself
continually nodding, tearing up, laughing, and checking for
my superhero cape. This book stayed on my nightstand until
the last page was read; I couldn't put it down. I'm left feeling
inspired and empowered by her words.

TSH OXENREIDER
Author of *Notes from a Blue Bike: The Art of Living Intentionally in a Chaotic World*

In *Surprised by Motherhood*, Lisa-Jo weaves together stories
from some of the most personal, meaningful moments of her
life, and I have no doubt that the Lord is going to use those
stories to encourage and minister to women at every stage
of motherhood. This book is a beautiful memoir of Lisa-Jo's
life so far, and her words are poetic, intimate, and thought
provoking. I'm not sure what Lisa-Jo's goals were when she
started writing this book, but I can for sure tell you what
she has accomplished: she has honored her family—and her
beloved South Africa—with her gratitude, her perspective,
and her deep awareness of God's faithfulness. I really do think
that when you finish this book, your heart will say, *Amen*.

SOPHIE HUDSON
Author of *A Little Salty to Cut the Sweet: Southern Stories of Faith, Family, and Fifteen Pounds of Bacon*

Whether you are a mother, know a mother, or have a mother, you need to read the words on these pages. Lisa-Jo Baker shares a story of brokenness and redemption, loss and gain, beauty and the messy process of becoming who you've been all along. What she shares will make you feel less alone, give you more courage, and open your eyes to see the divine right there in the middle of your anything-but-ordinary life.

HOLLEY GERTH
Bestselling author of *You're Already Amazing: Embracing Who You Are, Becoming All God Created You to Be*

From the moment I started reading this book, I fell in love with it. Lisa-Jo's stories are not only hilarious (because all of us moms can so relate!), but they are also raw and real. Reading about her unexpected journey into mothering and how she's learning to embrace the messy, hard moments it brings inspired me at a deep level. Hands down, this is one of the best mothering books I've read. Highly recommended!

CRYSTAL PAINE
Founder of MoneySavingMom.com and author of *Say Good-bye to Survival Mode: 9 Simple Strategies to Stress Less, Sleep More, and Restore Your Passion for Life*

Lisa-Jo is a writer who captures the beautiful essence of motherhood right in the middle of the mundane tasks. In this book we travel with her—around the world and through her journey into mothering, where she finds an unexpected and holy calling. As I read, I not only shared a long, intimate conversation with a friend, but I also stopped often to savor a sentence beautifully crafted and graced with insight. I highly recommend this book to every mother. A story of one woman's discovery, but really of all of our roads—through surprise to joy.

ALEXANDRA KUYKENDALL
Mom and lead content editor of MOPS International and author of *The Artist's Daughter*

I cried my way through this book. Lisa-Jo's words on motherhood and her story of her own mother-loss are both heartbreaking and dear. In these pages you get a glimpse of a girl stretching into womanhood, struggling against expectations, and trying to find her way as her mother slips away. It is so much more than a motherhood book—although that it is—it is also a deeply moving memoir. Grab your tissues—this one is a must-read.

SARAH MAE
Bestselling author of *Desperate: Hope for the Mom Who Needs to Breathe*

Surprised by Motherhood is an achingly beautiful tapestry of loss and hope, despair and redemption, that sweeps across the globe from the mealie fields of Zululand to the snow-covered American Midwest. Lisa-Jo Baker combines a deeply touching story with vivid prose to create an irresistible memoir that will have you wiping tears out of your eyes one minute and jumping for joy the next. This one is a must-read.

JENNIFER FULWILER
Author of *Something Other than God: How I Passionately Sought Happiness and Accidentally Found It*

This is the finest book on motherhood that I have ever read. Hands down. With breathtaking prose, Lisa-Jo Baker takes moms by the hand and leads us straight into wonder, which we can find right next to our dirty dishes, Cheerio-strewn floors, and overflowing diaper pails. This book is rocket fuel for weary mamas. I am recommending this book to every mom I know.

JENNIFER DUKES LEE
Author of *Love Idol: Letting Go of Your Need for Approval—and Seeing Yourself through God's Eyes*

Surprised by Motherhood is filled with grace, comfort, encouragement, sympathy, and laughter for moms in the trenches of motherhood who long for someone to come alongside and whisper, "I understand" and "All will be well." Lisa-Jo weaves her personal story of motherhood in a way that will live in your heart long after you read it.

SALLY CLARKSON
Bestselling author of *Desperate: Hope for the Mom Who Needs to Breathe* and *The Mission of Motherhood: Touch Your Child's Heart for Eternity*

Lisa-Jo is a welcome friend for any mama, at any age and season. Her warm, compassionate spirit reminds us we are not alone. A comrade on the front lines, she offers words that call out our best selves as we cherish and steward the years gifted to us. May we mother with our whole hearts.

REBEKAH LYONS
Cofounder, Q Ideas and author of *Freefall to Fly: A Breathtaking Journey toward a Life of Meaning*

surprised by
motherhood

everything I never expected
about being a mom

LISA-JO BAKER

mother | superhero | tea drinker

Tyndale House Publishers, Inc.
Carol Stream, Illinois

Visit Tyndale online at www.tyndale.com.

Visit the author's website at www.lisajobaker.com.

TYNDALE and Tyndale's quill logo are registered trademarks of Tyndale House Publishers, Inc.

Designed by Jacqueline L. Nuñez

Edited by Stephanie Rische

Published in association with William K. Jensen Literary Agency, 119 Bampton Court, Eugene, Oregon 97404.

All Scripture quotations, unless otherwise indicated, are taken from the Holy Bible, *New International Version,*®*NIV.*® Copyright © 1973, 1978, 1984, 2011 by Biblica, Inc.® Used by permission of Zondervan. All rights reserved worldwide. www.zondervan.com. (Some quotations may be from the previous edition of the NIV, copyright © 1984.)

Scripture quotations marked NLT are taken from the *Holy Bible*, New Living Translation, copyright © 1996, 2004, 2007, 2013 by Tyndale House Foundation. Used by permission of Tyndale House Publishers, Inc., Carol Stream, Illinois 60188. All rights reserved.

Scripture quotations marked RSV are taken from the Revised Standard Version of the Bible, copyright © 1952 [2nd edition, 1971] by the Division of Christian Education of the National Council of the Churches of Christ in the United States of America. Used by permission. All rights reserved.

Library of Congress Cataloging-in-Publication Data

Baker, Lisa-Jo.
  Surprised by motherhood : everything I never expected about being a mom / Lisa-Jo Baker.
      pages cm
  Includes bibliographical references.
  ISBN 978-1-4143-8785-7 (sc)
  1. Motherhood—Religious aspects—Christianity. 2. Mothers—Religious life. I. Title.
  BV4529.18.B33 2014
  248.8'431—dc23   2013045363

Printed in the United States of America

20   19   18   17   16   15   14
7   6   5   4   3   2

For my mom, Jo,
who was always going to write a book.

For my husband, Peter,
who was never afraid of my story.

For my children, Jackson, Micah, and Zoe,
who helped me find the words.

And for my Savior, Jesus,
who I believe would have loved me the
same whether I ever had children or not.

contents

why I wrote this book:
because you are my people

I GUESS MOST people who write books about motherhood start out by telling you how much they always wanted to be a mom. That is not my story. At sixteen, I was a skinny South African teenager with a crush on the tall, lanky swimmer who rode a motorcycle and left me roses. When I was seventeen, my mom was in the hospital and I was trying to figure out how to cook roast chicken while the pastor's son laughed at me all barefoot and cliché in the kitchen. When I was eighteen, my mom died and I swore I would never have kids. At twenty-one, I fell in love with a boy from the American Midwest with cowboy-green eyes, and at nearly twenty-five, I married him, on the condition that he wouldn't expect me to produce children.

More than a decade later, we have three. There's also the dog and a hamster. This is the story of how I got from there to here. *Here* being a sleep-deprived, messy rental house where I've discovered three things about motherhood. One, motherhood is hard. Two, motherhood is glorious. Three, motherhood is hard.

In between, there's a lot of sleeplessness, laundry, and diapers. And I'm still such a newbie. At this moment, Jackson, my oldest, is about to turn seven and lives for tae kwon do summer camp and flexing his biceps in our full-length mirror. Our middle, Micah, is four and a half, weighs more than his brother, and will lay you low if an animal is ever harmed in his presence. The baby girl, Zoe, arrived just over sixteen months ago, and my heart will never acclimate to the daily awe of rediscovering myself in her deep-sea-fishing-blue eyes.

Somewhere God is grinning. I can hear Him saying, "I promised you so" over and over again. How He always saves the best till last, and each new baby has seen me unwrapping unexpected treasure again and again until I'm laughing too and agreeing. Yes, the best. The very best. Even at 2 a.m. with the rivers of projectile vomit. Even then. I wouldn't trade it.

But I would do some things differently. I would throw away the parenting books that made me feel like I was somehow failing this most important test of womanhood—being a mother. I'd throw out the advice about what I was doing wrong or should be doing differently or should aspire to be doing. I'd just revel in the daily, sleep-deprived merry-go-round and eat a lot more chocolate cake.

Also, I'd go up to tired moms dragging screaming kids through Target and give them flowers. I would stop each and every new mom I ran into with chocolate and promises that they could do it. I would tell them they're my heroes—for every month of pregnancy, every 3 a.m. feeding, every boo-boo kissed, every diaper changed, and every plate of food they never got to eat hot.

I'd be tempted to break into song. But since I always forget the words of any song I try to sing and am notorious for just making up whatever pops into my head, my new plan is to write to them instead.

Sweet, exhausted, amazing, resilient, fearless, remarkable, run-down mom—this book is for you. No matter how you got from there to here, can I just take your precious face between my hands, look deep into your sleep-deprived eyes, and whisper, "You are much braver than you think"?

You are my hero. Someone needs to say it out loud, and I'm happy to be that someone.

Would it be weird to say I think about you late at night? When I'm rocking Zoe in our old, white rocker with the faded-yellow, Desitin-stained cushions, I'm thinking about all those mamas working the midnight shift. I'm thinking about all of us who are dancing our babies back to sleep or waiting up for them, like every generation of mothers before us—the ancient two-step that tattoos our love into the carpet, the hardwood, and the bosoms of our children.

Tired we may be. But also victorious. You are a wonder. What you do—it amazes me. You've got this. Even on the days when you think you don't. When you can't imagine one more shift. When you want to take off running after the ice cream truck. When you can't remember when you last washed your hair. When you want to climb back into your pre-baby body and the days that didn't start with Elmo and end with bathwater anywhere but in the bath.

You've got this.

This book is for you. And for me.

This book is for us.

Lisa-Jo Baker

NEXT TIME I'D DO MOTHERHOOD DIFFERENTLY.

I'd just revel in the daily, sleep-
deprived merry-go-round and
eat a lot more chocolate cake.

motherhood is a superpower

HARDWARE STORES USED to intimidate me. All those aisles of wood—two-by-fours or four-by-eights or ten-by-twelves—I have no idea. It's like an entire store full of math. And math has never been my friend. The rows of glue and tools and things that require electrical wiring skills are only somewhat more intimidating to me than the men who work there. In their gruff orange aprons, they seem to be able to smell estrogen from a mile away, and I've always been sure they would shut down any communication attempts at the first whiff. Nothing terrified me more than having to ask where the air filters were. I'd rather have walked laps around the store than be forced into admitting my sense of deep confusion and desperate need for storewide GPS to make it out with my dignity intact.

The gym could make me feel the same way. Stocked with so much big equipment that fit, sweaty people who don't at all look like they need to be there in the first place seem to know intuitively how to use, these places have always struck me as a clubhouse I'm not cool enough or brave enough or fit enough to enter. My friend Katherine could tell you about the time I showed up at a gym in an outfit that screamed, "I have no idea what I'm doing here" and sneakers that added, "I've never been on a treadmill in my life and would prefer to go back to walking the mall, where I belong." I did one obligatory circuit before I hightailed it out of there and didn't return for a decade.

It didn't matter that I'd gone to law school, worked overseas in jobs with big titles, or been through a bunch of passports, or that I spoke several languages; I always felt ridiculous anytime I entered either a hardware store or a gym.

But then I gave birth to three human beings.

Not all at the same time, mind you (although it sort of felt that way the first time around). I grew a baby and pushed him out and lived to tell the tale. And a few weeks later I walked into the biggest, most macho super-trendy gym in our neighborhood. I walked past the rows of workout machines. Past the aerobics studios and stationary spinning bikes. Past the pool and the warm-up area and the indoor track all the way into the deep, far recesses that housed the gym equivalent of a "man cave"—the weight room.

I walked in wearing pink and just stood there. I surveyed the landscape of muscles and testosterone and weight-lifting hulks, and I didn't blink. At home in my brand-new, brave body, I stood and let the rush of assurance run through me that I wasn't afraid anymore. I had scaled Everest. I had run with the bulls. I had shot the rapids. I had bungeed with the best of them. I had done something that required a kind of strength none of the men in that room could imagine, let alone replicate.

I just stood there and let the braveness seep all the way through me, and in my mind I might as well have been Kate Winslet, with arms spread eagled over the tip of the *Titanic*, yelling, "I'm flying, I'm flying!" And it was true. Just with much less glamor and a lot more call for nursing pads.

It was like discovering a superpower—becoming a mom for the first time. It has led me to believe that motherhood should come with a superhero cape along with the free diaper bag and samples you get when the hospital sends you, otherwise defenseless, home.

• • •

But the feeling fades. It fades under the mounds of laundry and more diapers than any of those pre-baby war stories could have prepared you for. It is threatened by the mundane reality that you will never be alone again. Ever. And that a baby would put an FBI tracking device to shame for the strength of its orbital pull on a new mother, who cannot leave the driveway let alone the neighborhood without what feels like years of planning.

So we turn to books. We buy bookshelves full of good advice from well-meaning experts who manage to make us feel even more tired than we did to begin with. Seven years ago, I thought there was a formula to parenting—you do what the books tell you to do, and then the baby does what the books tell him to do. I'd aced college and law school and figured motherhood would go down the same way. It turned out my baby had completely different plans in mind.

Motherhood became the first test, other than federal taxation, that I thought I was truly going to fail.

I would read all those books that tell you when the baby should be sleeping and when the baby should be eating and when the baby should be this, that, and the other thing-ing, and all I would see was a big, fat red F. Jackson did nothing according to anybody's schedule but his own.

And he threw up a lot. I would finally get him to eat, and he would look at me deadpan, cough, and puke it all out again. Forget crying over spilled milk, I wept over what felt like oceans of baby puke.

Wept.

Parenting is not for the faint of heart. And it's especially not for those type A personalities accustomed to having all their ducks in a row, all their check boxes checked, and their sofa cushions, cereal boxes, and entire lives neatly arranged.

I had a nursing chart. I'd harnessed my elementary school poster-board and marker skills and set up a timetable. After each feeding, I would dutifully put a check mark in the box—which side I'd nursed and how long—before I stumbled deliriously back to bed. Jackson cried, I nursed, I made check marks, and he never, ever once slept or ate as much or as long as the books promised my chart and me he would.

F, F, F, F minus in parenting.

I pretended it made sense to me. I pretended I had a handle on his "routine." I pretended I hadn't started to resent all those parenting books lining the shelves of our teeny one-room cottage.

And still he ate at a snail's pace and woke up to eat slowly at 11 p.m., 1 a.m., 3 a.m., 5 a.m., and 7 a.m. I kept waiting to fall in love with him, and instead I just felt like we'd both failed our midterms.

There was an afternoon when a friend came over for tea. (We do that a lot in South Africa. It's one of the best customs ever—early-morning and late-afternoon hot tea and cake or cookies or pie or rusks—our version of biscotti. And it's genius, I tell you. Genius.) Jackson was passed out on a milk high in my arms, and Natalie had two kids wrapped around her ankles. I was desperate. I was up-since-five-on-a-cold-South-African-morning tired, sore, and desperate for a formula that would give me back my old life.

I had been living with one foot in my stay-up-late, sleep-in-late, come-and-go-as-you-please world and one foot in my I-want-to-be-a-mother-if-the-baby-would-just-leave-me-alone world, and I wanted something to make the commitment to motherhood easier. I wanted the baby to adore me. I wanted to be the mom on those billboards with the beautifully blow-dried hair, lying in bed with one cheek resting against her cherub as he beams up at her. I wanted Jackson to want me for more than my milk. I wanted him to care about my feelings. I wanted him to wrap chubby arms around my neck and declare his undying affection for me and my sacrifices in front of smitten strangers. I wanted him to feel bad for all the puke and the laundry and the fact that I couldn't remember the last time I'd actually been out to a movie theater.

I wanted the baby to love me with such unbridled, adoring passion that everything I'd lost along the way would be worth it. Especially my size 6 jeans from Prague.

I didn't know it then, but I was grieving.

I was grieving the loss of a stage of life I'd loved, and I needed directions to navigate into this new one. A life where everything was unfamiliar and often scary. A life that couldn't be reduced to a poster-board checklist. A life that was mundane and unpredictable at the same time.

I stared over the top of Jackson's blond head and asked Natalie, "But when will he *love* me?" That one question carried all the weight of a mom half out of her mind with exhaustion and confusion.

And from the way Natalie paused and how gently she answered, I think maybe she understood everything I wasn't saying. She read the billboard over my head and quietly answered, "What you're doing now—all of it—that is what will build the love." I thought about it. I thought about every wake-up, every diaper change, every bottle, every single step of pacing to rock him back to sleep, every thankless load of laundry, every extra shift of cleaning up all the food I'd just fed him.

We drank tea in silence for a while. Kids played. Jackson slept.

The parable of motherhood is a profound one. I just didn't know it yet as I spooned more sugar into my Five Roses tea, passed the rusks, and wondered if time spent visiting could have been better spent sleeping. I didn't know that I was being grown up by this baby who had spoiled all my alone time. I didn't know that you continue to labor long after the baby is born. I didn't know that there was someone connecting the cacophony of dots that spelled out my life, which so far had seemed without rhyme or reason.

I walked with Natalie down the flight of stairs and rows of framed family tree photographs to the top of the steep driveway that rolls downhill and away from my parents' front door. The jacaranda tree was blossoming—a purple rain— and we hitched babies on hips and hugged good-bye one armed. Jackson was awake, and I felt ready to go another round.

A mother
continues to labor
long after the baby
is born.

CHAPTER 2

why you can't possibly know what to expect when you're expecting

I WENT INTO labor at around midnight in South Africa during an ESPN basketball game. We were up that late because midnight is the time they broadcast American sports in their entirety in South Africa, and my homesick husband was craving a little NBA. While he was up late watching sports, I was soaking my whalelike physique in the bathtub—the only way I'd found to take the edge off feeling like I was carting around several watermelons on my insides.

We were living in a small cottage in my parents' backyard, and Peter was downstairs in the main house while I was in the blue bathtub. I was as relaxed as only a clueless, first-time mother can be and enjoying the water, the weightlessness, and the crickets chirping outside. There was a hint of jasmine in the air, and I was about to heft myself up and out of the tub and off to bed when I heard a loud popping sound. I stood up with the excitement of the uninitiated to see if my water had broken, but that is not an easy thing to judge when one is already standing in an entire bathtub full of it.

So I got out and dried off and kept trying to peer over my bulbous middle to see what might be going on in the parts below that I hadn't seen in quite some time. All seemed quiet on the home front, but I figured I'd waddle down to Peter anyway and update him on what sort of felt like it might have happened, because that's what pregnant women do—we give our husbands a play-by-play on every iota of every odd sensation, twinge, craving, or imagining that goes on in us for the nine months it takes to grow a human being.

So waddle I did—down the windy little backyard steps cut into the side of the hill, where our one-bedroom thatch-roof cottage was located, and in through the back door, past the wall of family photos to the far end of the lounge, where the TV was whispering sports scores because everyone else in the main house was asleep.

You can probably imagine Peter's excitement at this non-development; I think he may have made eye contact with me, but the Bulls or the Lakers or some team was playing and he was pretty focused. So I lay down on the sofa across from him and wondered why my stomach felt so upset, since I didn't remember eating anything out of the ordinary for dinner. The bathroom was quite a waddle away, so I just lay on the sofa trying to ignore the discomfort growing within me. But nature would not be ignored, and after respecting its call, I found that my belly still hurt, along with my lower back.

Over and over again my stomach cramped up, and I lay on the sofa watching the basketball game and thinking to myself that if these Braxton Hicks contractions were anything to go by, I wasn't going to make it through the real thing. I lay there and contracted and pretended to watch sports with Peter. After a while those Braxton Hicks became so bad I had to snap at my husband to "turn off the sound, for goodness' sake" and breathe slowly and deeply to make it through each one.

Throughout my pregnancy I'd worried that I wouldn't recognize real labor once it started, but I was reassured by many well-meaning folks that I most surely would. I'd just like to take this moment to say, "I told you so," because for two long hours I was utterly, naively, and painfully oblivious to the fact that I was in pretty strong labor.

At 2 a.m. when I was breathing through clenched teeth and experiencing irrational waves of hatred for ESPN in general and the game of basketball in particular, Peter became convinced that it was time to go wake my dad. My father has been a family doctor for forty years, and I'd never been happier to be related to him than the morning of August 23, 2005.

He came down in his white T-shirt and boxers and knelt beside me with his long, lean limbs and bare feet. Then he placed firm hands on my taut belly. Watching my face, he asked, "How long has this been going on?"

"About two hours," I said as I lay wondering why on earth

I hadn't gone to a class about breathing techniques, because in that moment, it seemed I had somehow forgotten even the basics.

"When do you think labor will start?" I huffed and puffed at him through clenched teeth.

This is the point of the story when Peter and I finally started to wake up from whatever blissful ignorance we'd been swimming around in, because my dad looked up from his hands and my stiff belly and said with no small amount of stress in his beautifully accented voice, "My darling, you're in active labor. You need to go to the hospital. Now."

Pete and I, still under the illusion that labor would be "obvious" and that we'd "know exactly when it was time," just sort of stared back at him. Someone may have dunked something in the background.

So my dad tried again. He turned to Peter and spoke slowly and directly to him. "Pete, go get Lisa-Jo's bag NOW. You need to go to the hospital right NOW."

Then we did what all new parents do. We made phone calls. Because nothing says, "This is the real thing" like getting to tell it to someone else. Well, Peter made the phone calls. I headed back to the cottage to change out of my pajamas and into real clothes. And to grab my bag. And to lean against the wall on my way there and back so I could breathe through each contraction. My husband, meanwhile, was calling his parents in the States to tell them it was go time. My dad, I discovered when I made it back downstairs, was also on the phone—with my brothers who lived in Johannesburg, about a forty-five-minute drive from our home in Pretoria. In fact, the two men in my life were so busy spreading the excitement that it took some growling from me to get their attention.

I remember the three of us standing in the stairwell next to the photographs with our family tree while my dad prayed. There were whole lifetimes of doubt and anticipation crowded into that moment. My dad in his boxers, me in the sweatpants that had defined the last few months of my pregnancy, and Peter with his 2 a.m. hair all thick and standing on end. My dad put an arm around each of us and prayed a welcome for the baby, and I thought my heart would burst with the wild joy of it all if my stomach didn't first. I wasn't afraid. It turned out I wasn't afraid after all. God had met his promise, and in that moment I was so full of excitement and joy I can still feel it in my memory, all but pouring out of me.

I may have tiptoed into my parents' bedroom and whispered, "Good-bye, we're going to go have a baby" to my fantastic stepmother and totally freaked her out. And then we were off in the old blue Mercedes and headed toward the hospital. Peter drove very slowly, and I tried to explain to him that slow was for *after* the baby was born. Fast was for now. Very, very fast.

• • •

My dad had called ahead to let the hospital know his daughter was coming, and they were waiting and eager, and I knew we were going to be a team. I am now convinced that labor and delivery nurses are in fact angels dressed in light-green scrubs. There was no indignity with them. There was only a deep reservoir of safety and assurance that we were all in this together. I still wasn't afraid.

Before the sun crested the horizon of the southern hemisphere, Dr. Shaw and her team of nurses would lead me in the long dance of generations of women before me. I knew they were there—all my sisters with their birth cries echoing down through the years crowding into a small, white, sterile delivery room in South Africa. In that moment I was becoming one of them, and I caught myself astounded at the out-of-body realization.

But then it was time to push, and the pushing lasted much longer than it should have. A tug-of-war birth that ended in forceps and a rush to rescue my son, who was entering the world via a stubborn back labor and posterior position. I would have him out and in my arms, and I didn't care what it took.

"We're going to need to cut, Lisa-Jo." Dr. Shaw was calm but urgent. "I know we talked about wanting to avoid an episiotomy, but we need to get him out now."

"Do it," I told her. "Do whatever you have to." Peter says I didn't sound soft or romantic or any of the other adjectives I remember but instead that I roared with the guttural voice of motherhood, "Jackson, come on. Come on, Jackson!" as I bore down and my team pulled and my son was dragged into the world.

When he finally came unstuck, he came out fast, like a

cork from a bottle—all wet and screaming and so very alive. This firstborn son of mine—they placed him in one grand arc from my womb onto my belly, and I looked down at the scrunched-up face of that tiny human and was born again.

It is one thing to read about and imagine the birth stories of a hundred other women; it is quite another to witness a brand-new being you have pushed out of your own body cough and gasp his way to a first breath as lungs that have never held oxygen before expand for the first time. It is one thing to understand with your head that man was made in his Father God's image; it is quite another to look into the crinkly eyes of a wailing infant and hear his cries soften as you whisper, "I'm your mama" and you see your own image imprinted over his profile.

It is sacred. It is bloody. It is real.

It is truth that climbs off the pages of Scripture and leaps alive into your arms when theoretical beliefs in a Creator give way to experiencing the act of creation.

It is the backdrop to any childbirth war story that might have terrified you for the previous nine months. It is truth that colors wildly outside the stark black-and-white lines of labor. It is the heart of the heart of motherhood. That sacrifice—this seeming indignity, this hard and aching moment—produces such joy.

The sun was rising as I stared down at him. This baby I'd spent my whole life dreading. His face was turned blindly in the direction of my voice as I kept repeating those three words I never expected to utter: "I'm your mom. I'm your *mom.*" And deep inside of me, the crater of hurt left over from losing my own mother and the joy of my womanhood in the same year closed over, and I was filled with an emotion I still can't quite put into words. It's a good thing I was barefoot already because I knew with all my lost-and-found self that this was holy ground we were standing on in a South African hospital at 7 a.m. on a Tuesday morning.

That was the beautiful moment—backlit by a sunrise, the ecstatic adrenaline of a new mother, the glory of an epidural, and Jesus in the room.

But as I would learn, motherhood is a roller coaster of highs and lows. And just a few weeks later I experienced the second real milestone in my motherhood, and it was far more mundane.

My loud family was all gathered in the dining room and sprawled out in the living room, probably eating melktert and reveling in the wonder that was our son. He was asleep, so it was easy to appreciate him through the fog of sleep deprivation. But something woke him before I could really enjoy the fact that he'd been sleeping. And when he started to cry, everyone turned and looked at me. I kept waiting for someone else to get him when the realization dropped into my world that it would always be me. I would be the forever one expected to go when he cried. When he got hurt. When he was hungry or tired or teething. When he took first steps and when he fell down and when he graduated college and when he got his heart broken. That would be all me. Me and his dad. And me.

And I nearly stopped breathing with the weight of it.

MOTHERHOOD:

when theoretical
beliefs in a Creator give
way to experiencing
the act of creation.

from zululand with love

BEFORE WE GOT MARRIED, I told my husband that I didn't plan to have children. I may not have put it quite as politely as that. But I was carrying around a gut wound of leftover childhood junk, and it had convinced me that I'd rather run away than have kids. It was a backwards coming-of-age story from there to a delivery room in Pretoria, South Africa.

Our DNA is born from our stories as much as from our mothers. Maybe they're the same thing. Both of mine started deep in the mealie fields of Zululand—now modern-day KwaZulu-Natal—in South Africa. I grew up on the stories of a young couple—a missionary/doctor/father and a brand-new teacher/bride/mother—learning how to speak Zulu and make stywe pap, the stiff porridge-like maize meal that's the consistency of Play-Doh and a staple of South African dishes.

I can still close my eyes and smell mangoes. I can still hear the cicadas and the hadida birds and feel the red dirt between my toes, no matter how far I've traveled away from my childhood. And it took a journey of three hundred miles and three decades backwards to write the story that ended in a delivery room in Pretoria and started in the heart of Zululand.

It was August of 1974, the season of South African spring. My father, fresh from medical school, and his friend Cliff were the only two doctors serving the Manguzi Mission Hospital, named for the abundance of mango trees that marked the area. South Africa is a place of dry heat except for this tropical heartland of the Zulu nation. Remote, rural, and echoing with the guttural clicks and lore of Shaka Zulu, Manguzi was a place where apartheid was only slowly encroaching at the time.

My young parents beat it back with nothing but their faith and the way they chose to live. In the heart of the community—working, praying, serving, teaching, doing life alongside. And over nine of those months, my mother's belly grew large and stiff as that stywe pap, and she swayed to the rhythm of stamping feet and voices joining in chorus across fields and in the chapel where my father preached on Sundays.

While the mangoes ripened, Dad was flown by bush pilot into the remote parts of the countryside to set up clinics under the avocado trees. He tells how he tried to control the rough airsickness of the bumpy plane rides by setting his sights on one scrubby thorn tree after another en route to the villages. More often than not, he lost.

Mothers would line up with babies strapped to their backs by huge felt blankets. Choruses of flies and voices filled the air. Vaccinations, medications, and large doses of empathy were distributed. Sometimes long lines of open mouths would form for the dental clinic, shots given one after another down the row until the nursing sister made her way back to the beginning to start pulling the numbed teeth.

But even in the face of modern medicine, sangomas swore that the spirits spoke to them and demanded sacrifice when a woman was barren or a child was ill. And the people paid. The people always paid. They paid the malaria and the TB; they paid the wealthy and those with white skin. They paid the government and the leprosy, and they still managed to retain pieces of themselves.

This is the story my parents delivered me into. Because you can stoop through the doorway of a smoke-stained hut and eat over a three-legged cast-iron pot using only your fingers as utensils as you share about the day—and for a moment, you can be family. Our moment lasted three years. And I was born into the heart of it.

I don't know if my mother was afraid to have me so far from home. I do know that she claimed the promise from Isaiah 65:23, that the chosen of the Lord "shall not labor in vain, or bear children for calamity" (RSV). And my dad tells over and over how on the day my mother bore down and delivered me into the world, first she stopped pushing.

As he stood beside her, his young wife simply stopped in middelivery of their first child. Just out of medical school, with only Cliff on hand to assist, he couldn't understand what she was thinking—this woman who would give me her name.

"Jo," he said. "Jo-babe, you need to push. You have to push. She's coming. It's time!"

And my mother, he says, smiled and waited before she bore down again and delivered me into his hands—baby catcher, father, missionary man. They say I screamed loudly enough for my stoic ouma—mother to my own mother—to comment about her first grandchild with the last name of her fiery son-in-law: "Yes, you can tell she's a Rous."

Only later, when I was in the yellow crib they had painted and safe under the mosquito netting, did he ask my mother why. "Why did you stop pushing?"

And ever since I was a little girl, my heart has raced at her answer. "Because I didn't want it to be over."

Since so much of my story with my mother was cut short, it has somehow soothed me to know that from the beginning she didn't want it to be over. Like a hand stroking damp hair from my forehead, she reaches out of the past to soothe my thirty-eight years with the reminder that mothers never want it to be over.

Even the hard stuff.

They may want it to stop. They may want to find room to breathe, to weep, to panic. But they don't want it to end— this delivering, shaping, cheering, loving, bringing life into the world.

• • •

In the meantime, my mom was not good at normal mom things.

She regularly burned dinner because she neglected to pay attention. She'd be reading in her bedroom while the three of us kids were watching *MacGyver*, and a stink would begin to rise from the stove. Eventually she'd come running down the hallway shrieking at us for not telling her and scraping the charred bits off the green beans.

But food was secondary to community. And Sundays were for guests. Our house was always full. Watermelons bopped in the swimming pool, and the mashed potatoes were piled up high on the dining room table next to the sweet corn. With my habit of sneaking ice cream late at night, dessert was sometimes awkward, and my mom would have a conniption fit—albeit a quiet one—that there was nothing but a single scoop left to go with the meringues.

But most of all, she made room for the people, so I never noticed how the house looked or what food she was serving. I saw how they all wanted to be with her. How loudly she laughed behind those owl glasses and how there was never an expected end time for people to leave.

People stayed. The kids swam. Watermelons were split for dessert.

But from my perspective as a mom now, I realize it was hard for her to pay attention to things like the food and the right time to pick us kids up from school. Living loud in the midst of a crowd came easily to her. Being one-on-one with a child or trying to embrace a memory-making moment—those seemed like work.

We'd wait under that scrawny jacaranda tree at the Willowridge High School front gate, and she wouldn't come. We'd wait and eat Nik Naks, and my friends and I would watch cute boys from under shy eyelashes. We'd wait and she'd pull up enthusiastically late, and we could smell the popcorn on her breath.

"You went to the movies without us!"

She'd laugh and deny it, and we all knew it was true anyway.

She constantly danced between her old life and her new. With the books and movies and stories that ran so thick and deep inside her, it was sometimes hard to find room for her kids. But on the days she invited us in—on those days it was magical.

When I was twelve, she took me out of school to go to the movies with her. I was so important I thought my skin might split. But I was careful not to scare her off. I was careful not to be anything but utterly grown up. We went to see Mikhail Baryshnikov in *White Nights*, and she wanted me to understand freedom and art. How art brings us all the way into discipline, but how within those parameters there is a world of free. And that is what makes it all the more rare and beautiful.

Or maybe that's how I remember what I was *supposed* to learn. Maybe all I saw was the tap dancing and the Russian ballet defector and the desperate plot to rescue him. I saw the sinewed muscles and the cost to becoming great at anything and the fear of not being able to live that legacy. I was scared and exhilarated and brave as I watched with my mom and we danced for a whole hour and a half together.

I watch that movie now and can braille my way back into the world that included a mother.

I watch it now and can understand how it was hard for her to give up so much of what she'd been—a drama major, an English and Latin teacher, a totally unabashed bookworm. She loved stories and struggled to find the balance between living them and reading them.

I understand much better now that I'm a mom too.

I understand because Jackson was just a few months old when the second or third installment in the Harry Potter series made it to South African shores, and I holed up for an entire day to read. If the book hadn't been so thick, it would have been easier to balance the baby and the bottle of milk and the novel across my lap all at the same time. I understand because I, too, walk the tightrope between my old habits and my new ones, and as a mom, I want to be present in mind as well as in body. Smartphones make it easy to pretend. I'm sure my kids smell popcorn either way.

I understand because I want to stay up till 2 a.m. reading a new book or talking to a friend or watching an entire season of *Friends* without having to pay for it the next morning. Without having to worry about a 6 a.m. wake-up call from an extremely chipper and persistent toddler.

I understand because who doesn't want to escape for an

afternoon into a realm where women go to the bathroom by themselves and don't need to narrate what they're doing while they're in there?

It's funny how having a mom and becoming a mom are so profoundly connected. For eighteen years, I had a mom. Then for the next eighteen, I didn't. And I won't for all the other years after that.

Eighteen years when they're your first feel like a lifetime. I guess they are. But because they were spent so inwardly focused, I missed much of what my mom was like. That would have been the next eighteen, right? Getting to know each other as adults.

There are so many gaps. So many questions I would ask her now over hot, sweet English tea and scones. Not the hard American kind, but the soft, fluffy South African kind, served warm with butter melting into them and a topping of apricot jam and whipped cream.

Most of her parenting these days comes through memories. There's so much I want to do differently. I must be a much harder critic than if we were sitting across a pinewood kitchen table comparing notes. But the memories are all I have to go on as I rewrite the story of motherhood for my own children.

My father, with all his flaws, has aged in my memory into the profoundly approachable dad he is now. We have continued to do life together, so it's easier for him to come out favorably in the balance. But my mother . . . I must search and sift and piece together scraps—scraps that might be unfair. But they're all I've got. They are my story.

She said things I wish she could take back. She said things I'm sure she'd wish she could take back. And they wriggle deep under my skin without my even realizing it, buried there for years before my own babies force me to dig them out.

• • •

I was sixteen, and it was the season of beauty pageants. We were in the old, green VW Passat station wagon turning onto Charles Barret Street when I hugged my knees to my skinny chest and told her, "Mom, when I grow up, I want to be Miss South Africa."

She looked at me and answered out of the deep well of her own insecurity: "My darling, I think you're beautiful, just not in that way."

I didn't know until then that it was possible to be a girl and not be beautiful. I didn't know there were two kinds of beautiful.

My grown-up self wants to ask her what she was thinking and in the same breath wrap both arms around her and hug her hard, whispering, "Mom, I always thought you were gorgeous."

I sift through the words and listen for the undertones of insecurity I will not pass on to my own daughter. *Dear God, please help me not to pass them on to my own daughter.*

We drove on in silence, and just eighteen months later she was lying in a hospice bed, her head wrapped in a faded pink scarf with threads of silver running through it.

I went to show her my prom dress. The kind of dress that looks good on a tall, scrawny girl. It was royal-blue velvet with long sleeves and a scooped neckline that dipped off both shoulders. And it hugged with a curve that gently outlined the potential of a nearly eighteen-year-old all the way to the floor.

I spun slowly.

I didn't know what she would say.

I loved her so much my insides ached. I stood at the foot of her bed and twirled. She had on the light-turquoise sleep shirt I remembered her wearing every morning as she stood in the driveway waving, dancing us off to school.

I waited.

And all the grief and joy and life I felt came welling out of her eyes. Four words. She said the four words every daughter longs to hear: "You are *so beautiful.*" And in the last room of a long hospice hallway, I saw myself as a woman for the first and the last time in the reflection of my mother's eyes.

One week after I turned eighteen, my dad came home carrying her small blue suitcase.

"Why did you bring home Mom's stuff?" I asked him. "She needs it."

He just stood in the doorway with tears running down his face.

I kept asking him long after I understood the answer. I kept asking him so I wouldn't have to hear his answer. And when I finally did, I took off running to try to get out of my skin, and I ended up outside at our swimming pool. I dove in with all my clothes on, while the sun shone so indecently beautiful on a day that should have felt anything but normal. No watermelons bopped, no kids laughed, no guests rushed around to make it to evening church in time. Just the Kreepy Krauly pool cleaner chugging along the bottom and the empty afternoon ahead.

I called Liza Murphy, and her mom drove over to pick me up. We made small talk, and I had no idea how to share such awkward news with anyone. I finally choked it out to Liza when we were alone in her room. Her mom didn't know until Dorothy, the friend I'd known since first grade, arrived weeping to find me.

Twenty years ago.

I could never have seen it then. That all these random dots would connect to map out the latitudes and longitudes of a life I wasn't lost in after all.

But moving forward is usually impossible without first going back. And the girl who swore off motherhood needed to unravel her story before she could make sense of the newborn sleeping in the crib next to her, surrounded by swaths of white mosquito netting.

MOTHERS MAY WANT TO FIND ROOM
TO BREATHE, TO WEEP, TO PANIC.

But they don't want it
to end—this delivering,
shaping, cheering, loving,
bringing life into the world.

CHAPTER 4

a great, big man
named chuck

SIXTEEN IS AWKWARD enough without having to talk to anyone about cancer. The daily school uniform didn't help either: knee-high gray socks, a gray woolen skirt, a white shirt, and a blue blazer with a tie in the winter. The light-blue dress with the belt that never hit at the right place was for summer. I went to public school, but like most schools in South Africa, mine had inherited the British system when it came to rules and dress codes. No makeup or nail polish or loose hair allowed. School was ordinary and clumsy, and so was I.

There was one time the year before my mom got sick when she took me for a facial. I thought I would die of embarrassment when I was left all splotchy and red, with my bangs standing self-consciously up from my forehead where the headband had held my hair out of the way. It wasn't special. We didn't bond. I was just furious with her for compounding my already awkward insides with a face to match.

She'd grown up uncomfortable in her own skin and seemed unsure how to help me across the threshold into womanhood. South Africa has eleven national languages and all the cultural coming-of-age ceremonies to match, but my mom and I didn't have the right words for this next phase. Maybe they would have come to us if she'd had more time to live the ordinary ebb and flow alongside her gangly, growly, shapely-as-two-fleas-on-toothpicks teenager. But the summer we were supposed to redecorate my bedroom teenage-girl style, she ended up moving permanently into a hospital room before we could put up the wallpaper border of delicate pink flowers we'd picked out.

The only place where I still fit in my skin and my words and myself was with the community we'd been part of since before my youngest brother was born. When I was growing up, church was a consistent, resilient heartbeat for our family—a Sunday morning and Sunday evening non-negotiable. After the evening service, all of us kids would race to the kitchen snack window for Provita crackers spread thick with butter and Marmite and sprinkled with grated cheddar cheese. Our Sunday nights were stitched together with hot tea and savory crackers and teenagers all pretending not to flirt with one another in the background.

There was one Sunday morning when my friends and I

snuck a loaf of the Communion bread after the service and each took a turn imitating the various styles of the church members who partook—our parents, the spinster auntie, the organ player. I can't remember who caught us, but I do remember that I was one of the few culprits marched right to the pastor to apologize.

Church was family camp with all my best friends, cupped in the crook of the Magaliesberg mountains every year for a weekend of swimming, zip lining, late nights, early mornings, and memories laced with snack shop runs and Bible study.

Church was my dad waking us up with tea and Bible readings every morning before school. Church was the endearing South African habit of calling all our friends' parents "auntie" and "uncle" whether we were related or not. Church was progressive dinners for our youth group hosted by Auntie Ruth and Auntie Grace; it was Ryan playing the guitar and Rudi teasing me and staying up too late to drink coffee and talking about everything and nothing.

Church was rusks and peppermint crisp pudding. Church was a love language that spoke peace and comfort and home over my childhood right up until that night when we were all gathered at the Reads' house after youth group, and I wondered why Uncle Colin looked like he'd been crying. Or why my dad looked like he was the reason Uncle Colin had been crying.

And then we started the drive home, and my dad gave us the news about my mom's blood cell count. We hadn't gone two miles before he had to pull into the parking lot of the Dutch Reformed church up the road because it's impossible to drive and comfort your children who are trying to climb into your lap at the same time. I'd never cried shameless before. We were shameless in our gulps of despair and tears and snot and that feeling of being sure you're going to throw up. The unreality of it was claustrophobic. But there we were, with the parking lot and the dark sky and the shadow of Lynnwood Ridge Primary School—all so utterly familiar—around us, and so many dizzying stars spread out like infinity across the Southern Hemisphere.

This was real. This cancer was actually happening.

• • •

Life shifted and rearranged itself into a pattern of Dad working while I played dress-up for real and tried to mother my reluctant brothers and make sense of recipes in between school and turning seventeen. My first attempt at mashed potatoes left them a soupy mess, me in tears, and my little brother Luke reassuring that they were just fine as long as you closed your eyes when you ate them.

My mom was now a forty-five-minute commute away, and I wasn't old enough to drive yet. Every other evening my dad would load all three of us up and make the trek to Johannesburg to visit her in the high-rise hospital, where we were strangers in a new world. She was smaller, but she was not diminished. We'd don masks and hospital booties and rubbing alcohol and try to laugh our way back into feeling normal again.

The walls of her room were papered with cards from friends from work and church and all the teenagers in my youth group. Bright yellows, greens, and pinks against a sterile white wall. Her window overlooked the parking lot and the winding road that curled around the hospital and back to the freeway far below. After we'd crammed weeks' worth of parenting into a few hours, we'd head back to the car and the one spot on our way out of the vast lot where we could see her distant window. My dad would put on the hazards and we'd pull over and get out in the dusk, the setting sun coloring the sky over Jo'burg as we waited for her light. It would blink on and off. On and off. That way we'd know which room we should be waving to, craning our eyes against the sunset reflected in that mirrored wall.

Then we'd dance—waving and laughing and doing the do-si-do with Dad—so she could make us out against the skyline from so far away. We'd dance and wave and ignore the tears dripping down on all that hilarity. Waving and waving at a blind, square window that framed our mother and all that was good and normal and right with the world.

We commuted to visit my sick mother in the evenings, while I feigned interest in eleventh grade during the days, and somewhere along the way, the church I loved got lost and tongue tied and started to focus on what I was wearing or shouldn't be wearing and the plans I wasn't making to grow up into a wife and a mother. No one could seem to find the words to comfort me. And I grieved for the people who were separated from us by a chasm of normalcy.

What surprised me was how embarrassing my grief was. I was already awkward in my own skin—tall and gangly with bones where there should have been curves. Add a sick mother to all of this, and sometimes a seventeen-year-old burns with a shy shame she doesn't know how to put into words.

Sympathy can be awkward too, because what teenager wants to be put on the spot? Relatives and well-meaning ladies from church come over and comment on your lack of cooking skills, tut-tut over how often you order take-out, when all you want is for the tall blond boy on the 50cc motorcycle to notice you. Teachers either try to make excuses for your tardy homework or tell you that your "home prob-lems" are no excuse for your annoying behavior in class. And still the cool girls flip their hair just so, and you are tired of hearing about cancer and watching a parade of wigs as your mom's hair falls out.

How does a daughter chrysalis into her new skin when her mother is slowly disappearing out of hers? How does a daughter find a way to exorcise her pain when people expect tears but consider temper tantrums impolite, when punch-ing walls is not something teenage girls are expected to do? It doesn't help for her to hear that young girls should smell fresh and beautiful when she's sweating away her nights and days in a desperate inner wrestling match of worry. The deodorant can't mask the dying that's going on inside. A daughter will grieve whether she's given room to or not, and it will likely be unpretty.

Grief comes in strange getups. I made no bones about letting it be known I wasn't interested in trading my brain for a career full of babies, especially when I felt up to my neck in this oppressive trial run. Then one Sunday after the church service, two well-meaning elders sat down next to me to see how I was doing. But instead of it being an encouraging pep talk, the conversation meandered into a backward warning from two men who took a teenage girl's angsty declarations against motherhood at face value. They wanted to be sure I understood that God expected me to behave in a certain way as a woman—that I was duty bound to marry and reproduce and that His love and approval were on the line.

I pushed and they pulled. Forced into this world of figuring out how to prepare and set the chicken to roast before anyone else woke up, how to negotiate with my little brother's teacher about the weeks of blank pages I discovered in his school notebooks, how to shop for a prom dress without a parent present, I was desperate for a guide, not an ultimatum. So I dug in stubborn heels and swore louder than ever in my head that I would never submit to the cliché they were describing. Seventeen years old and lost without a mom to lead me on the sacred pilgrimage into womanhood, I felt ambushed. In the space of those fifteen minutes, I lost years of the joy of being a woman.

Somewhere around this time, the son of close family friends taught a Sunday school class about the fall of Adam and Eve. Except that he seemed to be particularly interested in Eve, since he was a medical student and had just that week attended his first baby delivery. Even today I remember his grim satisfaction as he described the wretched experience to a room full of seventeen-year-old girls. He'd witnessed the very wages of sin for women, he said—the Curse in all its painful reality. A woman who gives birth at the near cost of her own life.

By then I was nearly a year into the journey of watching my mother die. I had never been out on a real date, never learned how to apply eyeliner, never figured out the nuances of putting together a cute outfit. I had never talked to her about sex or childbirth or what being a woman beloved by God and her husband looks like. I had only just been kissed and was growing out my straggly bangs. And that day in Sunday school I was sitting with legs crossed and arms crossed and heart crossed between some of my best friends as we waited for our teacher to get to the hope, the climax, the happily ever after of the story of being a woman.

But it never came.

No whisper of the teenage mother who safely, courageously, and in defiance of her culture and her church gave birth to the Savior who would redeem everything I was in the process of losing.

I never told my mother that story.

When I visited her, we'd catch up on the ordinary bits like homework and teachers and school, and I never once told her how confused I was by what my church had started preaching. My mother's faith was always the Polyfilla cramming into any cracks in my belief. I listened to her talk to God, and I knew He loved her, this woman with the scraggly wisps of hair. I knew He heard her. Even when all she could get out was a whisper. Especially then. My mother's faith, like her flair for the dramatic, had imprinted on me early, and there was no separating it from my DNA.

In the eighteen months of my mother's illness, there were about three weeks when she was home from the hospital. I remember one afternoon during this time when I was late to watch a swim meet. My friend Claudette and I had made red cheerleader skirts with white polka dots over layers of tulle, and mine still wasn't quite finished. I was going to cheer for the boy of the motorcycle and first kiss fame, and I wanted one afternoon of normal.

I stood over my mom as she sewed. I kept my eyes on that old, enamel-colored machine we'd dragged out onto the pinewood table—the one with the extra flap in the middle that could unfold for Sunday hospitality. The house was quiet except for the machine and my mom's cough. She'd sew and I'd wait, and she'd cough into her handkerchief a blood-red polka dot pattern of her own. She stitched together an afternoon for me that I'll never forget. The skirt, the ride to the pool, the boy, and how he held my hand too long when he was saying good-bye. I cheered that day till I was hoarse, my aching throat a memory of something good and normal that couldn't be erased overnight.

• • •

I was going to turn eighteen, had my sights set on law school, and still didn't know what to do with my makeup.

A deacon's wife offered to take me to the mall, and I immediately said yes. I was delighted to have a mother figure interested in me.

When we pulled into the parking lot, she turned off the engine, looked over to where I was sitting, and said, "I hope you're not embarrassed to be going out in public with someone so much older than you."

I was surprised and quick to reassure. "No, no, I can't remember when someone last took me to the mall. I'm so excited—this will be fun." And I absolutely meant it.

She looked down at her lap and back at me and quietly said, "I'm sorry to say I don't feel the same way." My stomach dropped.

I listened in wide-eyed amazement as she gave me a quiet lecture about how I was responsible for what went on in the heads of teenage boys. And that the knee-high boots I was wearing embarrassed her.

"With your mom away, I understand that your dad probably doesn't have time to pay attention to everything," she said. "And I'm guessing he doesn't know what you're wearing."

I didn't know how to respond. I thought about my dad and how he'd winked and whistled as I'd spun for him, delighted in my attempt at fashion, before heading out. How he'd bought the boots himself for the teenage daughter who had fallen in love with the romance of a pair of shoes.

It was hard to find a corner of my womanhood that didn't make someone feel uncomfortable. Myself most of all.

Then my mom died.

My dad went half out of his mind with grief.

And I ran away to America and to college and to a place where I could be more than just the daughter of a dead mother. I had so much to prove, mostly to myself. It was comforting to be surrounded by an ocean of people who were starting over—all of us homeless freshmen learning to take first steps all over again, this time without our parents.

The whole time, however, I was strapped between an invisible sandwich board that declared in silent capital letters to the men around me, *MY BRAIN IS MORE IMPORTANT THAN HAVING YOUR BABIES.* A defiant sign to be wearing at a Christian college where marriage was practically a major. So it was pure serendipity when I met a boy who was fascinated by my brain. Quiet, unassuming, American, the quirky kind of funny, and someone who had all these real-life conversations with God as if He could actually hear us, Peter became my best friend.

My best friend who knew the story of my mom dying. My dad remarrying too fast. My dad divorcing. And my determination in the midst of everything to be defined by my degree, not by my uterus. Peter listened to it all. He always listened. It was a cherry blossom spring in Washington, DC, and nothing I shared scared this Midwestern boy with his green eyes and his passion for pizza.

So the next fall, when he moved to Boston, where I was finishing up my senior year, we were invested in each other, even though I swore I was not, and did not know if I would ever be, ready for marriage. What a charming peach I must have been.

Church ran as deeply in Pete's veins as it did in mine. So Boston found us looking for a church home on the North Shore and him picking me up at my dorm in his tattered old Ford Tempo every Sunday. That church in Melrose, Massachusetts, was warm and smelled like welcome. It had red carpets, wooden pews, and a greeter who used to remind the congregation crammed into that small building each week that "we just want to love on you." The expression has grown roots in my memory. How they loved on us—this anonymous couple so new to the dating dance who mostly sat near the back and left before anyone could connect too much or too deeply or too uncomfortably. I think we used to hit Pizza Hut on the way back to campus.

But not one Sunday. One week we were sitting on the far right, about three rows from the front. I don't remember anything about the sermon or what songs we sang. I don't remember if it was cold out yet. I don't remember if we put any money in the offering that day. But I know that Peter was sitting on my left and there was a big black man sitting right in front of me, partially blocking my view of the pulpit.

When the service was over, as we were struggling back

into our coats (so maybe it was cold out, after all), he turned around and introduced himself as Chuck. I shook his giant hand and was horrified when he told me that he thought he had a message from God for me. I was trapped into smiling politely and nodding yes, sure—feel free to share what I'm sure will only be a debilitatingly awkward encounter. Who wouldn't want that?

Chuck looked from me to Pete and asked if we were married. We shook our heads no, tried to hide the embarrassment. But he was quietly persistent. He apologized for any awkwardness but pressed on and asked if we were engaged. Again an awkward no. But still he persisted and wanted to know if we were planning to marry. I think Peter may have nodded—I can't remember clearly because it was a moment of such vulnerability. But then he asked in the gentlest and most tender voice, "And if you get married, are you planning to have children?"

At this point my sandwich board and I wanted to be swallowed up by the floor or take off running or ask Chuck who he thought he was or tell him what was really going on in my mind. But instead of blurting out, "I'd rather eat glass than have children," I politely, quietly, firmly said, "No."

Chuck seemed relieved. His big shoulders relaxed and he leaned in toward us, and looking straight at me, he said, "I think God wants you to know it doesn't matter to Him. God wants you to know that whether you ever have children or not, *He loves you for you.* And what He wants most is for you to love Him back."

I couldn't breathe. My chest was in the grip of a giant hand that was squeezing my rib cage, my insides, my heart. Tears burned down my cheeks—a silent but persistent affirmation of Chuck's message. But he wasn't done. Even though I wasn't looking at him anymore. Even though I was fascinated by the floor and my throat felt like I'd swallowed a South African summer.

"And tell me," he said, "did you grow up in a church that put a big emphasis on having kids? Am I right in thinking they told you that you had to have kids for God to love you?"

I nodded. And I could smell the jasmine and hear South African accents and feel my way back to being seventeen and lost. My hands were just as clammy as then but with much less bravado in this church so far from home.

"God wants you to know that it doesn't matter to Him if you ever have kids. He just loves you for you."

And I believed him. My chest loosened, and I could breathe again. And the gulps of air tasted like Truth.

Chuck turned to Peter next. God had a message for him, too. And it's a testament to Pete's character that despite my sandwich board and Chuck's message, he ultimately ended up marrying me.

"God wants you to know that if you marry her, it has to be for her and not for the babies she might give you one day."

I think Peter was holding my hand at this point. I think he nodded, serious, and told Chuck yes, he did know. He'd known for a long time.

Love, like hot chocolate, can warm us from the inside. We

saw Chuck and his wife only one other time after that—for a long, late Sunday lunch. But when we metabolize love, it can sustain us for years. It feeds the parts of our hearts we didn't know were starving. This never-giving-up, always-chasing love that isn't afraid of all the resentment a teenage girl can pack into two clenched fists. This lavish love that loves us first. Not because of our kids or our marriages or our tidy houses or our all-caught-up-on-the-laundry days. This is a love that loves because it can't *not*.

"This is real love—not that we loved God, *but that he loved us*."[1]

This love that teaches us how to love "because he loved us first."[2] This love that is so much like a mother's.

Love, like hot chocolate,
can warm us
from the inside.

two funerals and
a baby shower

MUCH OF MY motherhood is defined by the journey between losing my mother and gaining my firstborn. It is not a sad story, although there are sad moments. It is a redemption story. Losing a mother doesn't happen in a moment. It takes years to appreciate the impact of what is gone. It takes missed birthdays and moves and haircuts and weddings and new jobs, and then one day a first grandchild is born and she isn't there for it. So many women make the journey to motherhood without a mom. Whether she's absent because she chose to leave or because she was emotionally unavailable or because she died like mine did, we all have to make sense of what that means for our own mothering.

And so my journey toward being somebody's mom didn't begin in a labor and delivery ward or before that when I married Pete or even when I started to make sense of how much God loved me. Instead, it started with my mom's memorial service in Pretoria, followed by her funeral nine hours away, in the heart of South African farm country in the wild karoo plains. The weather was indecently gorgeous on both days.

The memorial service was held in the early afternoon of September, and my brothers and dad and I were getting ready in a fog at home when Uncle Alex arrived. This grizzled best friend of my father's had been like family since the two of them met in school and at seventeen canoed down 1,200 km and thirty-five days of the Orange River. The left side of Uncle Alex's face is set in a paralyzed grimace after a motorcycle accident when he was in his midtwenties that sent him into an oak tree. There isn't an ounce of pretense in this friend close as a brother.

We'd grown up on the stories of Dad and Uncle Alex. Camping, canoeing, skipping school, getting detention, farming—all the tall tales that turned the eyes of kids wide with wonder. And I can still see the two of them silhouetted against a campfire, stamping, dancing, acting out for us the legendary stories of Shaka Zulu and his wartime consigliere, Mgobozi.

Alex blew into the kitchen where we were trying to decide if we were hungry. The world felt like it was underwater, and it was hard to stand up, impossible to make decisions. But Alex arrived, and the tide receded with his coming. So much life bristling in our kitchen with his hard, beautiful Eastern Cape accent. We sat around that old pine table that had made its way from the Cape to Pretoria as he cut hunks of bread, spread out meats and cheeses and tomato slices, and fed our empty parts. I didn't know I was hungry until he arrived. Being around Uncle Alex could make anyone feel brave. He didn't offer sympathy; he cut and spread and dished up and served and loved us in the most practical way—with lunch. It was a lifeline. The house exhaled, and we were no longer one person short.

Alex chivied us along and we ended up dressed and fed and tucked into our car on the way to the church. There were slices of cheddar and avocado and uneaten crusts left behind in the kitchen, along with our self-pity. I wore the soft, black suede boots that came up to my knee and all the way past my self-confidence. I wore them in defiance of death and other people's opinions. I wore them because they made me feel brave and alive. My dress was a soft gray black with a delicate white swirly pattern that fell gently below my knee. I wrapped my waist with a light-brown deerskin belt, and that afternoon I was utterly comfortable in my clothes and my skin.

When we arrived at the church, there were already friends at the front door. Dad said this was a job we kids could do—greeting people as they arrived—while he finalized preparations for the service. So for the next forty-five minutes, we didn't move from that spot. As more people arrived, my brothers and I kept our arms open and stood outside the entranceway, black slate tiles beneath our feet, blue sky watching above. We hugged and held and listened to testimonies about how our mother had impacted a lifetime of people, many of whom we'd never met before.

There were nurses and orderlies and doctors. There were teachers and translators and teenagers. There were far-flung cousins and aunts and uncles and so many languages all echoing the same message—how beloved Jo was in all her ordinary extraordinary life. How she'd poured it out in high-rise offices, for patients at my dad's medical practice, for kids in my youth group, for the ladies in the old-age community where we'd served up plays and poetry readings led by my mom. How she knew all her nurses and doctors by name and family and story. How she'd lived and, even more, how she'd died with the courage of a hero, rivaling any of the characters from those books of hers I'd inherited. We stood and greeted receiving line–style, and only the color of the clothes would have warned a passerby that this was a funeral and not a wedding celebration.

By the time we made our way into the sanctuary, there was hardly a seat left to sit in. I found one with my friends. I think Dad and the boys were together more toward the front. The details are blurry. The music of one old piano and a congregation of familiar voices cemented into my memory forever. Dad spoke about his wife. His Jo-babe. She'd known she was dying, so they'd had time to plan together—one last time. She'd chosen the plain pine of a humble Jewish-style coffin. It looked so approachable up there in the front of the church.

Everyone around me cried. And I stood as we sang the hymn she'd chosen for us—for the ones left behind. I sang it with heart and stomach and soul full:

When peace like a river attendeth my way,
When sorrows like sea-billows roll;
Whatever my lot, Thou hast taught me to say,
"It is well, it is well, with my soul."[1]

And like every single Sunday I could remember, after the service was over we poured into the courtyard for tea. I don't think I drank any. Or had time to eat any of the beautiful snacks provided—the melktert and koeksisters, the rusks and banana bread. There were so many people to talk to. So many people who needed to share their memories and their loss with us. There was barely time to be sad. That would come later.

It was a glorious day. I was buoyed by the love of my people and how they'd loved my mother. Even then we recognized the strangeness of it—how we were a nucleus of joyful peace driving home in the green VW Passat.

A day later we were back in that car, headed the nine hours along the N1 from Johannesburg, past the gold mine dumps on the outskirts of town, all the way down to the Groot Karoo—a flat land of dry veld and windmills, Dorper sheep, and every holiday memory from my childhood. We were making the trip we'd made so many times before—to the sheep farm that had been in our family for generations, located between Middelburg and Witkrans mountain. Only this time we towed behind us a borrowed trailer with a coffin.

Before the appearance of the travel rest plazas that populate that route now, we used to stop under the shade of the acacia trees at designated picnic areas, with their white-painted rest tables and chairs. When Grandma Rous made the trip with us, she'd pack a large, rectangular Tupperware container with cucumber sandwiches cut into delicious triangles. There would be drumsticks and chicken breasts and everything sprinkled with shredded lettuce that we'd dip dirty, childish fingers into for second and third helpings. Then Mom would fold the backseat of the station wagon flat to make perfect sleeping quarters for the kids. With blankets and pillows piled all around us, we'd sleep away the barren scenery, and it always pained our parents that we didn't pay more attention to the wild beauty we were passing.

The road runs from Johannesburg in the north following the N1 through Bloemfontein in a straight, unblinking line down to Middelburg—literally, a town in the middle of nowhere. And for all my travels to Prague or Kyiv, Budapest or Rome, it is this barren stretch of earth that has become my plumb line for natural beauty. This vast emptiness—a sky that yawns down on you and a horizon you can see for days, pockmarked only by the occasional windmill or mountain.

Karoo dust still runs in my veins.

But for this trip there were no sandwiches, no real rest, and the only stop I remember was when we crossed the Orange River. Dad parked the car and the trailer on the side of the road, and we walked down to the muddy water. The sun was watery, and we were all starting to slip on the slow tide of sadness coming back in. Pulled back to the place of his beginnings, with no buffer of politeness necessary, Dad started to unravel ragged. He seemed to have run out of words to comfort anyone, himself especially.

This river of dreams was all run out for him now. We tripped on its awkward stones and knelt on the bank, and no prayers came. No courage. No laughter. No stories of how he and Uncle Alex had passed this very spot with just two canoes and no other company for weeks on end. We made our pilgrimage to the water, and all that it felt was pointless. From where we stood, I could squint back into the sun and see our car and the trailer parked behind it, and instead of standing at the edge of the Orange River with us, my mom was lying cold at the side of the road in that rolling coffin with its orange and white reflector stripes painted down the sides.

We crossed the Orange River into familiar country and could not have felt more lost.

There was a one-room undertaker's building in Middelburg that agreed to keep the coffin overnight before the funeral, the owner insisting he was happy to do it for free. We would come back for her in the morning.

The day of the funeral dawned, and I had no idea what to wear. I changed and changed again and kept digging into my suitcase, but nothing that made sense came to the surface. I wanted to wear something of hers, but all her clothes were too big for me, and Dad was calling, impatient. I wore her blue shirt anyway, with the shoulder pads and tiny white polka dots. It was way too big, and the belt I'd meant to keep it in place with wasn't in my stupid suitcase. So the shirt shifted and tugged and irritated me all day, and the pants I'd chosen kept slipping down, constantly needing to be hitched up.

Back at the undertaker's, they led us into a little room closed off from the rest of the space by only a thin curtain. The coffin was brought in and laid on a table in front of us. We wanted to see her. The coffin hadn't been open at the memorial service, and it wouldn't be open at the funeral. But her husband and three children wanted to see her one last time.

The floor of the place was bare cement, and all these curious laborers who'd helped move the coffin were just hanging back, waiting for the lid to open. I felt the rush of emotion heat up my back and down my arms and flood my face. One of the men had a screwdriver in his thick hands and was prying the lid loose.

"No."

I was bellowing, but all that came out was that soft, one-syllable declaration. I put both hands palm down on the pinewood and said it again. "No."

Then, in a strangled whisper: "No, everyone needs to go out. We need to be alone."

But they'd heard me. And they shuffled out in their overalls past the filmy curtain, letting it fall back into place. A token act of privacy.

Then Dad shifted back the lid. It was Mom, but of

course it wasn't. I stood and looked and loved her—my tiny, shrunken mother. Someone had put a soft, pink woolen cap on her bald head. Like you might put on a newborn to protect her from the cold.

And then we were loading up again and driving the forty minutes out of town into the greatness of the karoo. There would be no more stores on our way to the farm, and anything else we needed would have to wait till we were back in town. I needed to stop at the pharmacy on the way out. Dad's nerves were shredded by then, and he wasn't patient, and my shirt didn't fit, and I couldn't tell him that I needed tampons. Funeral or not, my body was on its own calendar. My mother was dead, and my body was relentlessly counting the days of my own womanhood.

The route from Middelburg to the farm is a lonely one. The road sweeps in a wide arc around the squatter camp outside of town before it straightens again and heads in a flat arrow toward Witkrans Mountain Pass. But before all that veld rises to the horizon, Tafelberg Mountain looms on the left. Literally translated from the Afrikaans as "table mountain," it shares a name with its more familiar cousin—the Table Mountain of Cape Town fame. Run aground here thousands of kilometers from the coast, Tafelberg marks the northeastern border of our farm. Most of my family has climbed to the top of it at one time or another, but I've always been content to crane my neck out the car window as we drive and drive and drive by it for twenty minutes or more.

Every holiday of my childhood was spent on this farm.

After a day of travel, when we would finally turn off the highway and onto the dirt road at the small green-and-white sign for Stradbroke and start the half-hour trek across the farm to the actual house, my dad would always let us kids climb onto the car's bonnet. It was the reward for hours shut up in cramped quarters.

I'm surprised my mom never minded. But we'd sit skinny butts down on that hot green hood and surf over the speed bumps every few meters. There was the tree, all knotted and knobbly, left at a strange angle after Uncle Jolyon drove into it late one night. There was the dry creek bed where we used to race the horses. There was the dam with the massive old willow trees that had buried their desperate roots deep into the cracked mud. There was the cobblestone Muratta Pass that cut down to the last gate you had to cross before you were actually on the driveway to the house. And then, finally, there was the Willow Pond on the right with surprised turtles leaping off rocks into the water.

I don't remember any of it the day of my mom's funeral.

One memory we were in the undertaker's back room; the next we were all gathered at the far end of a pasture known as Meerkat Vlakte, watching a coffin being lowered into the dry dirt. In a surreal twist, the undertaker had provided us with a batch of bright green Astroturf to lay around the hollow grave. He'd told my dad it would make the dust more manageable. Those nearly neon strips of green, utterly out of place in the khaki browns and yellows of the karoo, said more about the wretched unreality of burying my mother than I could find words for at the time.

We were desperate observers, my brothers and I. Along with a small group of people who shared so many of our Dutch genes and guttural accents, we watched as my father crippled under the agony of this final good-bye. I stood on the far side of the grave with my brothers and watched as my dad, on the other side, bent at the waist with his weeping. Gasping, his hair blowing in the dust, his hands holding on to the knees of his pressed suit pants, he wept. I was so worried he would fall over. The green turf at his feet, the escarpment behind him—that first shovelful of dirt undid all the parts of him I used to recognize.

Working alongside the men of the farm as he'd done since childhood, my dad shoveled dirt and wept until Stuurman, the big Zulu foreman, laid a gentle hand on Dad's back and took the spade out of his hands. They finished up without him. And when we turned and headed back to the cars all parked along the fence line, I read the enormity of what had happened in the pale, shocked face of a relative who tried to make small talk. Ashes to ashes and dust to dust. There is nothing romantic about it.

● ● ●

It was five years before I visited that grave again. Peter was with me, having asked for a plane ticket to South Africa as his only graduation gift. We drove the red Opel Astra up to the fence and climbed through the wire at the far side of the camp, where the headstone stood outlined against the small hill, or koppie, in the distance. I wanted to lie down on the grave—a primal urge to do a breaststroke in the dirt. Instead, I only knelt by her side. Knelt and traced the words cut into the rock headstone:

> Therefore we do not lose heart. Though outwardly we are wasting away, yet inwardly we are being renewed day by day. For our light and momentary troubles are achieving for us an eternal glory that far outweighs them all. So we fix our eyes not on what is seen, but on what is unseen. For what is seen is temporary, but what is unseen is eternal.
>
> 2 CORINTHIANS 4:16-18

It was Peter's first trip to South Africa. We'd traveled thousands of kilometers and so many accents to introduce him to all my family. I knelt in the dry veld and was too shy to lie down and cry like I wanted to. Terrified at how raw and unattractive my grief might be if I let it come screaming out.

I didn't want him to take any photos of the place. Holy ground covered in the droppings of dassies—the hardy rabbit-like breed that lives in the veld and its rocky outcrops, their hard-to-spot burrows making it dangerous for galloping horses. By the time we headed back, donkeys were nuzzling the car—three of them, with grainy yellow veld grasses up to their knees, sticking their nosy muzzles into the windows we'd left open.

The sky was hard, bright blue—so much life framed in those wide-open spaces. The air was a portrait of home. Windswept dust that smelled of sheep and meerkats and cattle enclosures. Fences you had to duck your head down low to slip between the wires. Peter in his Timberland boots and American accent following me into all these beautiful, hard places.

Maybe my mom had seen us coming. Maybe she had been waiting. Six years earlier on a Thursday in May, she'd written me a letter in her looped and flowing handwriting about making sense of living in this in-between.

How I remember you on your very first morning with Grandpa's cross mouth—yelling defiance and hunger and waving your fists. You have grown more precious to me every minute since.

We shooed away the donkeys and, laughing, piled back into the car. My little brother Luke, with all his long, lean limbs, folded up in the backseat next to the boy who would become my husband. Dad driving us all out of the past and past the milking kraal and over the iron grid, crossing back to the road that wraps around the front of Stradbroke farmhouse. He'd sold it along with the farm after she got sick, to cover the medical bills. We drove past the sweeping green lawns and the fishpond and the water reservoir where we all used to swim despite the algae.

*I think my sickness is like God with a loudspeaker
saying to the Rous family, "Wake up! Look up! There's
more to life than netball and cooking and computers
and rushing to the library and drama practice and TV
and movies and cleaning the pool and being head girl."*

We drove past the overgrown orange and apple groves on
the right and the lush pockets of lucerne on the left that the
horses would munch after a long ride if you'd let them as they
clip-clopped the last yards home.

*There's eternity—where are you going to spend it?
And don't you want to start living eternal life right
now? Because you can—you don't have to die physically
to be born again. We can belong to the Kingdom of
Heaven right now—and it can make a difference.*

We kept to the right and headed back up the rocky pass
to the long dirt road and the highway beyond. To the left
were the red barns and sheep-dipping pens and a thousand
stories of Dad and his brothers and sister working their days
away between the bleating ewes separated from their lambs.

*That's what I think God is giving us a second chance
to prove—how living as King's kids, as citizens of
the Kingdom of Heaven now—can make all the
difference in our lives and in the lives of our friends
and neighbors.*

With windows rolled down and dust in our noses, we waved past the bulk of Tafelberg on the right and the dry dam on our left. Dad told stories about Indwee the Blue Crane that would dance with Grandpa Rous, and we laughed and sailed over speed bumps, keeping eyes peeled for springboks and baboons.

What do you think of all this? Write or phone and tell me—I look forward to hearing from you. My specialest, darling daughter.

When we reached the highway and turned left on the blacktop, the car picked up speed again, headed for Grahamstown and my mom's family. The unchanging karoo comforting in its hard barrenness. I was wide awake for this trip.

LOSING A MOTHER DOESN'T
HAPPEN IN A MOMENT.

It takes years to
appreciate the impact
of what is gone.

because sometimes becoming a mom is like moving to a foreign country

PETE AND I finished out our final year in Boston, and I was still sure I'd never want kids. We completed three years of grad school in South Bend and married in the shadow of Notre Dame, and I still couldn't imagine changing my mind. We moved to Chicago and then to Ukraine. And it was in the post-Soviet city of Kyiv where I slowly, haltingly learned Russian and that there was a secret wish for a baby growing in my imagination.

I turned thirty, and all I wanted for my birthday was the one thing I'd been avoiding as long as I could remember. We were living down the road from the famously red Shevchenko University in an apartment building on Gorkoga Street, nearly two years into Pete's stint as a State Department fellow in the former Soviet Union. Many days it felt like we'd stepped into a black-and-white movie. Neighbors went door-to-door to whisper in Russian that *Americans* had moved into the building.

I learned to hail a cab, haggle over vegetables at the market, and order bread in the language they call God's own because it takes an eternity to learn. And on my thirtieth birthday, we sat outside at the Golden Gate Café with a smorgasbord of desserts and flowers and the sun so beautiful on an August afternoon, with the two missionary families that had adopted us and taught us important life skills like how to order take-out pizza in Russian. And in that moment, I knew there was only one gift I really wanted.

Bob and Colleen, Cliff and Heike, and their five kids between them were unexpected family in a country that could have been crushingly lonely. From miles away in Florida, Pete's Grandma and Grandpa Hamilton had introduced us to these missionaries who had passed through their church once—naturally they'd kept in touch and kept praying for them. Letters and e-mails were exchanged, and eventually airline arrival times and invitations to connect made their way into the correspondence. When we arrived, they pulled us through the looking glass and into their stream of life and work and worship and showed us how to survive the months when the hot water is shut off while the pipes are being cleaned.

But the day we arrived in Ukraine, Bob forgot we were

coming, so Peter negotiated us through a sea of black leather coats and a language that swept over and around me and into a taxi and then a hotel that required us to hand over our passports as part of the check-in procedure. A nightclub throbbed on the lower floors until sunrise, and we stood and watched the Dnieper River, which cuts the city in half, change colors under a foreign familiar sky.

Cliff picked us up at the hotel after Pete's various phone calls in broken Ukrainian to the Skinner apartment and then to the Wright apartment and then to the church office finally turned up someone who had heard we were coming. And Cliff brought us on a Saturday afternoon to the place we'd be most likely to bump into everyone he thought we should meet: he brought us to church.

The first time we walked through the front door of the converted apartment building on Studentska Street, Lesya was coming out. In her arms was newborn baby Lisa. Ukraine was ushering in a late Indian summer, and life was all around. Babushkas were unpacking the donations sent from faraway churches and delightedly putting any kid they could get their hands on into hand-me-down Britney Spears T-shirts and college sweatshirts with teams and logos in English they couldn't read. So many Sundays over the next two years we would sit in those wooden pews and understand almost none of the sermon but all of the Spirit of the place.

Recovering addicts and alcoholics; mothers, kids, and teenagers; Lesya leading worship with her husband, Sergei; their two older kids tucked into pews with friends; and me holding baby Lisa. Peter played drums, and we both kept time in that unexpected place. Colleen on her guitar sang words I'd known for years and only fully understood when I heard them in that language I couldn't understand—that language that made everything sound like faith.

In Ukraine no one demanded that Pete and I have kids. No one pressured. No one peered into the whys or why nots. They simply anticipated. They loved us, and we could feel their delighted anticipation that a marriage they were so fond of would naturally walk its way into parenthood.

In the meantime, I watched Colleen and her three boys and their crazy black dog always on the go. She enjoyed them. More than that, I would say she *reveled* in them. They came with her and Bob across borders, on Soviet trains, and into markets, apartment communities, and churches. They didn't slow her down. They were part of her journey. They breathed Russian, they translated for visiting international teams, they played chess and made movies on their computers, and they watched their mother living wildly outside the lines of quiet or tame or ordinary.

Colleen with her big blonde hair, long skirts, huge smile, and fearless mothering was a first for me since my mom died. It's hard to quite put my finger on what makes Colleen so fierce in my memory. She would be up at crazy hours making birthday cakes or Easter cakes or writing cards and notes to members of the congregation. But it wasn't because she loved to bake or craft. The *people* inspired her. Marshrutka drivers and next-door neighbors who came by in their shouty

Russian and housecoats to discuss the electricity being off again. To meet her was like reconnecting with a long-lost friend. She would throw her arms out wide to welcome strangers. Her laugh was loud, and her enthusiastic embrace of the culture they were living in was contagious. Like me, she had no white picket fences in her memory. Slipping into the nooks and crannies of her every day gave me a taste of family again with a woman at the center. A woman who was filled up by filling her home with people.

Now, two years later, she and Bob drank Coke across from us, and their boys ate their way through ice cream, and as far away from South Africa as I was on my thirtieth birthday, I found I'd come home. In this hard-to-live-in country where drinking water is carried by five-gallon containers, where a currency and a culture are slowly recovering from the beating of Communism, I met a woman who was brave and capable and whose children were integral to her calling.

Pete and I had been married for five years by the time I turned thirty in Ukraine, and for two of those years, Colleen had been rubbing off on me. With her big bangs and bright lipstick, she was comfortable in her skin. She was her own self, and spending time with her helped me feel more like myself—safe in my own skin, comfortable with my story. I slowly shared the broken parts with her over tea and hard biscuits. My hair grew long again in Ukraine. I learned Russian. I wrote grants for USAID and the EU, watched the entire ten seasons of *Friends*, and started to think about becoming someone's mother. I had distance, and with distance came perspective on my family. I could see the shades of parenting and grief from afar, and they didn't seem as scary.

I wrote a letter to my dad. The more I thought about having a baby, the more I knew I wanted to wipe the slate clean for this new human being's beginning in our family. I wrote to him about what I'd lost as a daughter in the church we grew up in. I sent my memories and words across two continents about the woman I'd grown into and the childhood I'd left behind. I started telling the story that I was writing with my life and this new beginning. I nested with words long before the days I would nest with scrubbing bubbles and paper towels. I plucked out old splinters. Smoothed off rough feelings. Laid new foundations, started fresh patterns.

For the first time Pete and I were gypsy equals. Both of us the foreigner. A neutral territory, Ukraine allowed us to discover a new way together. How to navigate the metro. Where to buy fresh meat. What a taxi ride should cost. No one had the home-court advantage, and it pulled us close and tight until we realized it might be time to share all this with someone.

And then one Sunday after church, Colleen asked me if we wanted to come over for lunch and spend time with some visiting friends who spoke English. We were in the sanctuary when she asked. The youth group leader was doodling with his drumsticks. Babushkas were still chatting across seats, and the teens were straggling in for their afternoon service. I'd been counting days for a month. So I whispered my excitement into her ear. I told her that I was ovulating and that lunch meant we'd miss an important window. How she laughed. How she clapped her hands in delight. How she grinned and grabbed me with fingers digging into my upper arms, hugged me, and told me to Get. Myself. Straight. Home. And have some great late-afternoon sex. She was so unembarrassed. Life all around us in that welcome church sanctuary—Colleen and God—how they made me believe motherhood could be good. So very good.

• • •

Some eight thousand kilometers away, the ground was leveling out under my father's feet too. Both of us learning to look at the hole where my mom had been and not keep falling into it.

My dad had married two years after Pete and me, to Wanda (pronounced Vuhn-da), an Afrikaans-speaking woman of action. The awkwardness of a new woman in the house lasted only as long as it took us to absorb the warmth of a home filled with people, food, and tender touches for all the kids—her two and my dad's three.

That white house built into the side of a South African hill had been lifeless for years. There was so much sad cemented into the rock walls, and it was a relief to have someone else in the space to defuse the tension. Wanda threw open the windows of the Honeyrock house, and life blew in again.

Late in the afternoon on the day of the wedding reception,

a minivan taxi had delivered to the foot of the steep drive-way of that thatch-roof house at least fifteen of the men and women she'd worked alongside for years at the Spar store in Hammanskraal. They came, and with them came the music. I was down the street hugging cousins good-bye—I think I was barefoot—when I caught the strains of Tswana voices lilting over the back wall. I remember running up the drive-way and then the front steps, worried it would be over before I could see it.

Past old family trees that lined the wall, I burst into the garden and a circle of stamping, clapping, ululating wedding guests, with Dad and Wanda caught up in the middle. Wanda, with her white dress hitched up in one hand and the bride-white tiger lilies in her hair, dancing to the irresistible harmony of new beginnings. It was impossible not to be pulled in by the friendly hands and the revelation that this woman who lived and breathed a language different from my own was rebuilding our home out of people.

She built with bricks made of family, vetkoek, and Five Roses tea in tall glass mugs, a fascination with all things cricket and rugby, massive Boerboel dogs, and supper around the big table with all the seats filled again. Wanda was so many fresh starts—it was how I imagine a good long pull at the inhaler must feel for an asthmatic. We could all breathe again. Dad was growing back into the best version of himself, and Pete and I felt good knowing he was being taken care of while we were in Ukraine. It felt healthy and enough.

And then? Then around the time I was just catching on

to enough Russian to safely catch the metro in Kyiv, Baby Karabo came into Dad and Wanda's life. And Karabo brought Tshepiso, Thabo, and Petunia. And Petunia would bring Lulu and Mo.

Years later, when Pete and I moved home from Ukraine and into the cottage in their backyard, my dad would tell me how all he ever really wanted was to be a preacher but how God kept giving him children instead. Like He'd always known that's where the gospel lives—in the messy chaos of opening up our lives to others. Wanda was the one who showed him how. She showed us all how.

Karabo is a Tswana name meaning "an answer." For Dad and Wanda, and for all of us, really, Karabo was the answer to many questions. For example: What can God do with the little we offer?

They had been moved by a particular verse in the book of James:

> Religion that God our Father accepts as pure and
> faultless is this: to look after orphans and widows in
> their distress.
>
> JAMES 1:27

So they asked a local social worker they knew if she would introduce them to families who needed support. Families of orphans. Families known starkly as "child-headed house-holds." The social worker set up home visits with several families. My parents planned to deliver care packages, food, clothes. They did not plan to begin an adoption journey. But then they met the first family.

You know how the story goes. Five thousand hungry people, no food or markets in sight. One little boy, five loaves, and two fish. And the rest is history. Except that it isn't. Because God kept multiplying and multiplying and multiplying what my parents had set out to do. He broke their expectations and offered them new ones, greater ones, more satisfying ones. He broke apart their plan and offered back His own, and it filled up spaces none of us knew were there until our family was eventually multiplied by one little boy. One little boy who brought a big brother and big sisters and eventually two nieces and an umbilical cord connection to the orphanage they all could have ended up in.

Wanda brought us all back to her roots. And those children who came from the place that was home to her for years began to grow in the hearts of so many of us living in far-flung corners of the globe.

One winter afternoon years later, when my family was visiting South Africa, we made the trek out to Hammanskraal with a convoy of friends from church. We pulled in to a dusty patch of dry grass in front of one of the orphanages to echoes of "Mama Wanda" from the playground that had recently been donated. She laughed and wiped her fringe out of her eyes and didn't miss anything.

Her compassion is not pitiful. It is hard and demanding. They love this about her. How she takes the time to instruct, to call out the cheekiness, to tease, to take girls to get their hair braided at the local taxi rank where it's the cheapest and the braiders are the most skilled. She wins them over, all big grins and fascinated eyes.

There were updates about the two sisters with the matted hair who hadn't spoken their native Afrikaans for years, so long had they been stranded in this house of Tswana vocabulary. There was talk of the plans for Christmas celebrations, the family that needed food and clothes. There were massive stainless steel pots of mealie pap being stirred by the aunties who parented this place, who opened their doors to the children who were used to being left outside.

The last building we visited that afternoon was bleak. A dust bowl for a yard and a pile of rocks that the little kids were running up and down and up and down while the big boys kicked a soccer ball. Wanda was carrying a snot-nosed baby.

My son Jackson was tired and came to find me, to find a bathroom. We stood in a room full of beds, and the boy who inherited my homesickness whispered so that I had to bend down to hear him. He whispered, quiet and desperate, "I don't ever want to live *here*, Mama." And I had to carry him around for the rest of the trip—his gangly legs wrapped around me, his hand shielding his eyes from the sun and a version of his homeland that was hard to look directly into. As the teenagers scored a goal in the background, we finally packed up the car again with the kids who got to come home with us. One or two of the others had to be gently, painfully picked up off the back again and again and transferred to the dusty yard.

Wanda knows each of these children by name. She sees them. She keeps coming back. Mama Wanda. Her hard blue eyes are not intimidated by what they see. Wanda, who has driven dark streets and desperate back roads for prodigals. Wanda, who lives the parable of adoption on so many levels it's dizzying. Wanda, who always, always comes. Who fights. Who wrestles. Who prays the prayer of the good shepherd and goes clambering after the lost one, two, twenty with food and warmth and the assurance that she will keep coming back. We follow her. We all do. We know her voice, serving, weaving, and praying that all things work together for good. Not just for happy endings.

• • •

Mothers are born from the strands of so many stories woven like DNA—tenderly, delicately, and sometimes painfully into this thread that runs through families. Colleen and Wanda, South Africa and Ukraine all stitched into my journey toward motherhood until I crept out of bed early one Christmas Eve and took the test that told the story of the baby who would first make me a mother. My favorite gift that year.

THAT'S WHERE
THE GOSPEL LIVES—

in the messy chaos
of opening up our
lives to others.

CHAPTER 7

there is no
road map

I CAME HOME to South Africa to have my firstborn as a peace offering for being away for a decade.

We had all the equipment for raising a child but no clue what to do with either. I was much more interested in scrap-booking adorable pictures of the adorable baby than actually staying up at night to feed said baby. I wanted to plow through the entire Harry Potter series, go to the movies, or make a run to the mall, and instead I found myself tied to a tiny human being.

And the tired—oh, let's talk about the tired. The bone-crushing exhaustion and the idiotic books that tried to tell me I should start my day at 5 a.m. when the baby started his and be sure to pump whenever he slept. I know much better now that what you should do at 5 a.m. is WHATEVER IT TAKES TO GET THE BABY AND YOURSELF BACK TO SLEEP.

It was daunting to leave the hospital with Jackson. Looking back at myself years later, I want to reach into the memory and take by the hand that girl who thought she'd be wearing her pre-pregnancy jeans home and gently assure her that there's no need to be embarrassed by the fact that what she actually ended up going home in were the same massive sweatpants she'd been wearing when she arrived. My jeans, my shirt, and my body didn't fit right, and my husband treated his first diaper change like we were defusing a nuclear weapon—all the equipment arrayed like a halo around Jackson on the hospital bed.

We came home just in time for my birthday. Jackson turned three days old; I turned thirty-one, and our church home group brought over dinner for everyone. I kept trying to find something to wear that would fit all the parts of me that didn't feel the same anymore. All my old clothes seemed unfamiliar. So I stuck to the soft black pants and shirt that had embodied my pregnancy even though the top button on the shirt now strained against my new curves. Jackson wore the white jumpsuit with the blue mouse embroidered over his heart. I rushed to get ready, rushed to dress and nurse and redress and change Jackson, and rushed to get Pete to wait, stop, stand right there before we walked down to the main house because the sun was setting just so and I needed one more perfect photo as proof of this new thing that had happened to me.

People kept arriving with food. Cars kept trying to Tetris themselves into a driveway so steep it's a stretch for three—impossible for more. My dad was hanging out the top window under the eaves of the thatch, yelling down parking instructions, offering to come and do it for them. Afrikaans greetings came ringing up to the window, and a line of women traipsed up the stairs and wrapped me in knowing hugs, their husbands shaking Pete by the hand, slapping him on the back. Both of us acting like this was normal, like we might really be able to digest this reality everyone was congratulating us on as naturally as the food they were delivering.

People *kuier* in South Africa—they visit for long, companionable stretches with no sense of urgency or clock watching. So the house bulged with conversation and endearments for our new addition. I wasn't sure who to be in this circle of beautiful attention. I was me, and I wasn't. They commented on how great I looked, and all I could think about was how much was hidden under layers of tender cotton. The ladies wanted to see the crib, the cottage, the setup of our new lives, so I walked them up and down the steps between my parents' house and our nook, and it hurt but I was oblivious because I was so enamored with being normal.

My brothers arrived in the mix, and the family started to get restless and hungry. It was quickly becoming clear that bringing over a meal for a young couple and their newborn requires a lot less food than bringing over a meal for a young couple, their newborn, and the extended family they lived with. The kuier and the cars and the accents finally departed down the long driveway, the table was set with food and hungry faces, and still Jackson had to be changed—diaper, clothes, and all—and then he had to be fed. So I sat on the sofa in the living room with him while everyone else dug in to my birthday dinner across the room, and by the time I was done and he was burped and finally asleep, there was no chicken left.

We lived in the thick of family as we tried to build our own three-legged version of home. Peter was struggling to write his PhD dissertation, and I was trying to play a role I'd read about in one too many parenting books. And every evening I hid in the bathroom as I slowly washed my beaten bits and pieces and tried to avoid my naked reflection in the mirror.

The cottage was one room with a loft for the double bed that looked down over the small desk, coffee table, dresser, and crib. The bathroom had always been my favorite since I'd lived there as a teenager. Tucked behind the only door, it housed an electric-blue tub, toilet, and sink—the color I always thought of as joy.

I was slow in the bathroom those first few days. Slower than Jackson liked. He was impatient, and one night Pete came looking for me, walking in on my desperate privacy. I recoiled from him. I yanked the door closed with both hands, bent over trying to hide my new self from the boy who'd known only the sexy version. Humiliated, I yelled. I told him not to look, not to come close as I clung to my camouflage. I was stunned when he didn't listen. My quiet Michigan man of few words pulled that door wide open and looked me in the eyes and said loud and clear what I didn't believe: "I think you're *beautiful*. Don't you ever hide your body from me. Beautiful, do you hear me? This is the body of my *wife*, the woman who gave birth to my son. You. Are. Beautiful. I love you, don't you *dare* be embarrassed in front of me."

That was the beginning. That was the beginning of being ready to be parents.

• • •

The thing is, there is no road map. No matter how many stories you've heard. No matter how many books you've read. It's learning to walk again, and the only way to do it is by falling down a lot. Because you're becoming someone else, and your stretched and broken skin can itch with the strangeness of it. But Pete had my back and my hand and an immovable version of me locked safe in his eyes, so I could trust this strange new life with him. And I discovered it smelled a lot like Elizabeth Anne's baby lotion.

Jackson would wake up in the darkest hour, and I would race down a curve of stairs from the loft to get to his crib below, always breaking out in a sweat when I heard his crying like an alarm siren ringing in my gut. Stranded in the middle of his dark cherry bed with its swaths of white mosquito netting, like some small pirate captain, he smelled of milk and Elizabeth Anne's. Every memory I have of motherhood is laced with Elizabeth Anne's, and I've ordered it from afar for my kids born stateside. I've brought cases of it back and forth between continents, and when I've traveled without my babies, I've lathered it slowly onto my own skin at night—a tender benediction to the body that bore them.

We couldn't figure out what kind of night-light would be dim enough for Jackson to sleep by and bright enough to change a diaper by, and we ended up with a makeshift lamp we hung three angel ornaments from, mobile-like. We'd bought them on a cold day at the tourist market in Kraków, Poland. It was our last trip without kids. We were retracing Peter's student days, and we bought ornaments for our Christmas tree that ended up entertaining our son during midnight diaper changes in a small cottage in South Africa. They swung from their perch above the changing table while we tiptoed around him as he slept in the same space we were living, brushing teeth behind a closed door and avoiding the step that squeaked.

During the day he had the place to himself for naps—the baby monitor would summon us from the big house when he was waking up. I have reels of photos of his mouth slowly curving awake—now he's yawning, now he's smiling, now he grimaces awake. I was his fascinated student, his lover, his slave, but only slowly, ever so slowly, his mother.

The books were full of how-tos for Jackson—how to get him to eat or sleep or burp or open up for solids. They were silent when it came to the how-tos for me. How to feel about this change, how to love this tiny tyrant, how to give up a universe of uninterrupted "me time," how to always, always have a cloth on hand for the moments when he would inevitably pee directly into his own face or mine during a diaper change. No parenting book spelled out in neat bullet points how to wrap my head around what I'd lost and, even more, what I'd gained. Some days it felt brave and fantastic; some days it felt like beating my way through the scrubby African bush with only a blunt machete and no sign of the horizon. At 10 p.m. or 5 a.m. or three in the afternoon, it was the same truth: the only way through is through. As much as we crave shortcuts or explanations or formulas, one day will end and another will begin, and it will be different until it isn't. Until it starts to slowly make sense and we've found our balance.

There was an evening when Pete and I were utterly lost in our attempts to calm Jackson, to help him sleep, to find our way out of a long day and into those few quiet hours when the baby went down. Instead, the baby just caterwauled at the world, and the walls of that small cottage closed in on us. We looked at each other, frustrated, and wondered why the other one couldn't figure out a way to make it stop.

Our front door was open, and summer dusk was seeping into the room. But because life was drowned out for us by our screaming son, we were oblivious and missed the arrival of my dad with a couple who wanted to say hello, to peek into our world. Our world blinked back, caught in the headlights, with wide, panicked eyes, and we didn't know how to even begin to make the scene look familial or welcoming. The woman oohed and aahed over the romance of our little "love nest," and the man stood in the doorway looking as awkward as we all felt. I shrugged my shoulders and tried to smile, Jackson kept screaming, and Pete looked like he wished he could leave with them.

Later, much later, I'd bump into her at church, and she'd give me another version of that evening. She said they'd heard the wailing of the witching hour a good way back before they knocked; they knew what they were walking into. They recognized the familiar chaos of a new beginning that stretches the sinews of the will, the heart, the eardrums. They weren't oblivious; they just had the advantage of a much bigger picture.

• • •

I'd washed each and every little bitty one of Jackson's baby clothes, added softener even, before we brought him back from the hospital. I think Gladys, who keeps my parents' house running like clockwork, had ironed the tiny tops and pants without my knowing. At six months pregnant, I'd tried to shift Great Oupa's massive bureau by myself. I'd bought a throw blanket for the maroon futon and painted the shelves built into the backside of the staircase white. I'd thought I was ready. I'd known myself well enough to skip out on the prenatal class where they watch the inevitable real-life labor video, knowing that for me, "what you don't see can't scare you" was gospel. But I'd really believed I was ready.

So when he'd developed jaundice the day after we got home and the nurse came to set up his little BiliBed with the blue lights that made him glow like a lowrider's neon license plate frame, I wasn't sure why she asked me how I was doing. And I wasn't sure why answering her with a simple *fine* came hard to say through a throat tight with tears. His delivery had been hard on me and hard on Jackson. He had bruises that hurt me—the imprint of the forceps clear as a child's fingers in Play-Doh down the left side of his face. And I couldn't get him to nurse enough to relieve the ache of my engorged breasts. I watched her watch me and read in her eyes the welcome message that I wasn't expected to feel normal at all.

I called Dorothy the next day. My friend since grade one, she and her husband, Carl, had also just made the move back to South Africa. She was one baby ahead of me. She didn't hesitate. She just hung up the phone and arrived fifteen minutes later with chocolate cake and a breast pump. Jackson was sleeping, and Dorothy fed me cake and hot, sweet tea as we sat in the TV nook on the squishy sofa while the sun through the glass door warmed up the parts of me that the tea and cake had missed.

It's a relief to know that motherhood is hard. This is the gift girlfriends can give one another—the 2 a.m. truth about parenting. How it can hurt and which pads or ointments or boxes of chocolates can help ease the ache. We talked and ate and then she walked me to the cottage, where Jackson was asleep, and showed me how to use a breast pump. Grace and chocolate cake can cover a world of awkwardness.

Becoming a parent is a lot like breaking up with yourself. There are all these things you used to love about yourself and your life. Those late-afternoon naps. Those spontaneous movie nights. The tidy house and pretty things that could easily break. Lots of pretty things. Unbroken pretty things. Uninterrupted meals, sleep, bathroom breaks.

Children arrive and blow through what used to be your routine. They huff and they puff and they blow your life down. You wake up at 2 a.m. because someone calls you Mom. Except they don't say the word at first—they only offer the wail, and you find yourself stumbling out of bed, groping for sense and the night-light, and in that moment it's over. The old you is left in the wake of washing out bottles and warming milk and walking five hundred miles of carpet.

There was one night at church when Jackson was fast asleep in his car seat, and my internal clock told me it was time for him to eat. Or maybe I just wanted an excuse to lift that delicious bundle of tiny corduroys and denim shirt into plain sight. Either way, he was a disinterested audience. Indecisive, I offered him a bottle and then figured I'd better find somewhere private to nurse him instead. It's what all the other moms were doing. Crowded into a small room with its one-way glass wall, hunched over infants happily gurgling down what they offered, everyone else seemed competent, calm, qualified.

I realized that the shirt I'd chosen wouldn't easily accommodate hiking it high enough for Jackson's head. I started to sweat. It was hot in that quiet room, and my son was loudly annoyed and impatient. I fumbled and readjusted and didn't know how to relax enough to help him relax, so eventually I gave up and went to find a quiet nook behind a pillar in the back of the church where I could quit judging myself. It still wasn't the greatest success, and eventually we found ourselves back where we'd started, with my returning him to his car seat where he gratefully went back to sleep.

But that was nothing compared to the night we took him to home group. Someone gave up his seat for me near the center of the circle of friends we were trying to make, and it felt like maybe it had been worth coming. Maybe the cold evening and the baby who had to be fed just so and changed so many times and packaged into his seat and the car and the effort not to get lost as Peter drove on the left side of the road to meet up with a group of people who all preferred a language other than my husband's might have been worth it.

They were entranced by Jackson. As his blue eyes goggled at all the faces of fascinated singles and young marrieds, I swung him up and down, up and down from my lap to high over my head. He loved it. Maybe everyone loved it. At least it felt friendly; it felt normal to show off this delightful side of a newborn. They didn't need to see the 2 a.m. frustration when he wouldn't eat more than a few ounces over the span of an hour. They didn't need to know how tight our living quarters were or how hard it can be to find your feet as a family when you're living with, and relying on, your parents. They didn't need to see our doubts or our demons, because they were staring at our son. I relaxed for a moment. And in that moment, when he was at the height of laughter above my head, Jackson vomited an arc of wet, goopy baby hurl directly into my face, down my arm, and slowly into my lap. It was incredible. And everyone saw.

I wanted a do-over. I wanted to go back home or back three years. I wanted to be anywhere but in my skin, and there was absolutely no chance of that. My skin was dripping. My clothes were soaked, and every eye in the room tried not to blink, to make eye contact with anyone else, because the unspoken look would have said louder than any words, "Dude, that is THE grossest thing EVER!"

Let's face it, that's what I was saying to myself. Awkwardly climbing over feet and guitar cases and holding Jackson like some kind of toxic waste stretched out in front of me, I followed the hostess into her bedroom as she riffled through her closet while looking from me to her clothes and back again, trying to convince us both that it would be no problem, no problem at all to get me changed and back to the group. But I knew we'd passed the point of no return.

I don't think I even bothered changing Jackson. I just asked her to get Pete and waited in the front hallway till he came and we could leave with our tails and our diaper bag between our legs and I could cry privately in the car.

• • •

I remember being embarrassed at sixteen. I remember being the last girl to start shaving her legs or wear a bra or figure out eyeliner or successfully navigate any of a whole host of other coming-of-age changes. And I remember how my mom would hold me and how soft and comforting it was to be pressed against her bosom. She'd chuckle and tuck my hair behind my ears and smile her crooked smile and tell me, "Oh, my darling, once you have babies, nothing will ever embarrass you again."

That truth was slow in coming. It had to burrow its way into my life, between the leftover college parts of me that liked to be beautifully put together and the insecurity of seeing a scrubby reflection of myself in some other young mom's eyes. Jackson grew me up and out of myself more thoroughly than any church service or youth camp or volunteer project ever could have.

Stripped of all pretenses, of all instinct for posturing, babies pull us into their orbit of naked truth. They are hungry, they cry, they throw up, they have diarrhea in the airport right before boarding. They disguise nothing. It doesn't occur to them not to say exactly what they're thinking. They take their first steps buck naked with hands stretched out and eyes locked with ours. It's impossible to look away, to go back, to stop growing.

Some days I still miss the Lisa-Jo I used to be. But those days are rarer than they were when Jackson was just a few months old. Like a pair of saggy old jeans on a Sunday afternoon, the word *mother* fits me more comfortably now. But there were days under the lilac jacaranda when I shook my head and couldn't understand how I'd lost myself in the wash and spin and rinse and repeat of new rhythms I couldn't find my groove in.

When I was single, I used to go out dancing with my friends. Give me a bass beat and a girls' night out, and I would lose myself in the music. I could rock myself to sleep on the beat of a night spent devoted to nothing but three girlfriends, mushroom hamburgers, and french fries at Ed's Diner. But this—this was a new rhythm, and my body was awkwardly fumbling toward the beat.

So I rocked and walked and soothed and wrangled my own confusion. And still I stood with one foot in the life I thought I loved as I waited for the baby I'd wanted to start to love me. Nonsense. I lived a lot of nonsense before life started to make sense again. But that's because the breaking up can be a slow process. And it takes time till you can keep time to a cataclysmic new beat. It takes courage to say no to yourself and yes to someone else. Over and over again—days, weeks, weekends, years, and trips to Chuck E. Cheese's on end. The way a gut-punch takes your breath away with the sheer shock of the change.

So I spun and spun in dizzying circles, until sometime just before Jackson turned one, there in the distance I spotted the small unremarkable speck of who I used to be.

And I waved.

As the dance swept me on.

Becoming a
parent is a lot like
breaking up with
yourself.

CHAPTER 8

what brave
looks like

Any way you cut it, motherhood is intimidating. From the courage it takes to clip a newborn's fingernails or navigate the weensy little arms into a Onesie or wave a child off to school, the ocean of a mother's worry is a vast one. And with each new baby, we are that much more vulnerable to having our hearts broken into tiny little bits of forever. So moms might not know it, but they are the bravest of the brave for taking this risk. Against all odds, knowing that sickness, sin, failure, and disaster lurk on the fringes of every day, we choose to embrace life. We open up ourselves—our bodies, our lives, and our futures—to the whims of another human being, and there is no going back. And perhaps what makes this kind of everyday courage the most remarkable is how very seldom it gets recognized.

Jackson toddled toward his first birthday, and our time in South Africa crashed to a close around our ears. Pete needed a job, and the closest one was in Michigan. So we packed up our lives, our memories, the cherry-red crib, our clothes, the leather sofas, my heart, and the desperate dream of South African roots.

For his birthday, Jackson's ouma and oupa gave him a red ladybug tent with a tunnel that attached to it, and he and Karabo camped out there for hours during the days leading up to our leaving. Their huge grins reflected in each other's faces—one the color of night, of chocolate, of home; one as light as his Dutch and British mother, as jasmine, as the snow we were headed back to. Jackson and Karabo. Karabo and Jackson. Nose to nose, head to head, hand to hand, they were destined for friendship before Jackson was even born. Lives and stories and naps and bath times all wrapped up into a singular memory. These two boys who told the story of our time in South Africa and the ache of our leaving more eloquently than my words ever could.

Jackson was wearing sweatpants striped like tropical candy canes when we waved good-bye at the airport for the last time. We'd presented our passports, received our boarding passes, and checked the last four pieces of luggage, the rest of our home having already been shipped the week before. I held our tickets in my hand and could hardly stand to raise it in one last wave before we walked away from my dream of homecoming and slipped between the check-in counters and through the tunnel toward customs and immigration. We stood stranded between two South African Airways ticket counters knowing this was it; this was good-bye.

I've spent what feels like years of my life in airports, and it is always terrible—the last look. And in that frozen moment, Karabo ran as hard and as fast as he could toward us, calling out Jackson's name. He ducked under the security rope and all two feet, sixty stocky pounds of him ran straight at Jackson. And Jackson spread his arms and his grin as Karabo barreled into him.

No one else moved. All the adults watched. The security personnel, the ticket agents, the parents, and the passengers stood and watched as two boys embraced across cultures and airport regulations and laughed and said each other's names over and over. And I grabbed hold of my faith with both hands, believing that the God who had made us family would bring us back to this place again for another homecoming.

As he's done every trip before and since, my dad had prayed over us before we checked in. I clung to those words as I looked at my firstborn son who would become a transplant in a new land before he could even string together a sentence. I know of no other recipe for making a good-bye bearable than the promise that the God who goes with us and stays with them will be the bridge connecting us, no matter how far or long the distance. So our boys hugged hard one last time before the adults intervened, and with grins through our tears, we all whispered across the distance, "Good-bye, good-bye" and in Afrikaans, "*Tot siens.*" *Till we see you again.*

• • •

Detroit was cold when we arrived. Pete's aunt Marcia had been waiting for us, circling the airport in the silver-gray minivan, and snow spit icy-hard in my face as I fumbled to buckle Jackson into his car seat. I think at some point we picked up sandwiches at Subway on our way to the small town of Owosso I'd visited just once before. My mind was frosted over, and I could only sit numbly next to Jackson and wonder how my story had unraveled so quickly. I was finally starting to fit into my pre-pregnancy jeans again, but life felt uncomfortable, hard, confusing.

The loss of homeland and family felt like a physical wound. I bled; I cried. And for months after the move, I felt disoriented and disconnected. I did not sense God in it at all. I walked forward in blind faith, stumbling over myself and my regret.

Pete's aunt and uncle took us into their home, and their daughter, Cora, gave up her bedroom for us until we could find our feet and a place of our own. I remember that Michigan winter of transition being so dark I could barely see my hand in front of my face. The old crib that all three Skjaerlund kids had used was squeezed into a corner of the room next to the bed Pete and I were sharing, and at all hours of the night, Jackson would stand up and peer over the edge, calling me over and over again. By 2 a.m. he was always squeezed between the blankets with us, and none of us got any rest. Pete left early for the job he was so grateful to have, and I tried to keep up on the work I'd left behind in South Africa—telecommuting from an Atlantic away, in the basement, with Jackson crying upstairs over a culture and a babysitter he didn't know.

American relatives kept calling to welcome us home. And there was a day I stood clutching the phone at the kitchen sink that wasn't mine with hands still wet from the soapy bubbles, and I let the angry sadness spill out into the open over a call with my mom-in-law. Telling her why this felt like failure, not homecoming. And like her son, she listened and loved me the best by accepting my sadness with both hands and not trying to make things better.

And then Jackson got sick. It didn't matter that he loved Uncle David's John Deere riding mower in the garage or the attention from the preteens in the house who doted on him—it was his body that got hit hardest by the transition. I don't know if it was the change in climate or food or air, but he caught a bug that rocked him through round after round of diarrhea and vomiting until we were spent. I'd spend my days with him draped limply across me in a rocking chair in front of the TV. Aunt Marcia followed us around with Lysol spray, and I was too exhausted to offer to help clean. I was fighting my own virus.

Homesickness is like fatigue. You feel vaguely uneasy and a little disconnected from everything. It makes you think you've forgotten something but you just can't remember what. It's the reason you think you recognize people only to realize just before you call out their names that it's the wrong country and so it couldn't possibly be who you hoped it was. And sometimes homesickness sprouts up out of nowhere like chicken pox, and it's best to try to avoid others until you are no longer contagious.

Christmas came, and we were supposed to be in Illinois with Pete's parents. Jackson's doctor advised against traveling, but there was a house available for us to rent in the New Year, and everything we owned was in storage with Pete's brother and sister-in-law in Wisconsin. We would do Christmas with his parents and swing by Chris and Jill's place on our way back to Michigan to pick up our earthly belongings.

We'd been two years in Ukraine, where we'd slept on a mattress that was little more than two wadded-up blankets. We'd been two years in South Africa, where we'd waited to send for the rest of our belongings until we were settled. We were never settled. It had been more than four years since we'd seen any of the furniture we'd bought when we were first married. Four years since we'd had anything permanent. And most of it was stored in Chris and Jill's basement. When we arrived out of the dark and cold of the Wisconsin night, they were up waiting for us.

I remember how well they loved us without actually using words. Because sometimes words are too difficult to hear.

Sometimes you're just not ready to dissect what you've been through. Sometimes you need both more and less than the words. Jackson was still sick as a dog, and we were adrift on the grace of others for what would come next. We had been sleeping badly for weeks and were anticipating an inflatable mattress or the couch.

Jill led us downstairs to the basement as I carried the deadweight of Jackson, resigned to a long, sleepless night of him throwing up and Pete and me taking turns to reinflate the mattress, wash him down, and try again for a few more hours of rest. But at the bottom of the stairs was home. At the bottom of the stairs was the bed Pete and I had bought as newlyweds and slept on for only two out of our nearly six years of marriage.

"I thought you might like to sleep on your own mattress," Jill said.

She'd set it up for us in all its king-size glory. Wrapped in fresh sheets and layered with comforters and blankets and down pillows, it was waiting for us. Something melted inside of me. Something hard and angry. As I put Jackson into the bed and sank down into its depths, something that had been crushing my heart shifted, and I could breathe.

All three of us slept in that bed for nearly ten hours straight, and everyone had more than enough room. That dark basement welcomed us into a place outside of time zones and failure, and the bed accepted us back into its bosom and rocked us through the night. Held in the embrace of family without a word being said. We may have bought that bed in

South Bend, Indiana, but it was given to us on a cold winter night in Milwaukee, Wisconsin.

•   •   •

We couldn't afford to buy a house or get much of a rental either, but family friends had a home they couldn't sell and were prepared to rent to us for a fraction of its worth in exchange for our being prepared to move out at a moment's notice if it sold. The place was deep in Michigan farm country and would have stood vacant if we hadn't arrived when we did. Pete's aunt and uncle lived down the road, across a small bridge and around the corner, and they continued to absorb us into their hearth and home even after we moved out into our own place. And slowly we started to find our feet and take tentative steps forward again.

I discovered that at the heart of my misery—beyond the homesickness and sense of failure—was a misunderstanding about faith. I had confused faith in God with faith in what God could do for me. I had been viewing God like a mystical vending machine: I inserted my prayers, pulled the handle, and expected the desires of my heart to pop out the bottom slot. It turns out God has very little in common with Pop-Tarts. And what makes me happy is not necessarily what draws me closer to the God who knows my every nook and cranny. It turns out He loves me enough to say no when, as every parent understands, saying yes would have been so much simpler, with less call for temper tantrums.

But that is where He met me. At the crossroads of His decision to move us away from South Africa and my final, grudging acceptance of it, He led me out of my heartache and into a season of redemption and beauty. All without changing His answer. Instead, He changed me.

Under a deep-blue sky and back roads lined with cornstalks taller than my son, in between neighbors who would become friends and a small-town grocery store where they always gave Jackson a warm cookie from the bakery, we slowly unclenched our fists. The sun didn't set until close to ten during the summer, and we would chase Jackson up and down the acres of deep, thick grass in the backyard until none of us could breathe—we'd all just collapse in a heap of tangled legs, his white-blond hair, and Pete's scratchy goatee and watch the first fireflies come out.

And then, after nearly a year in Michigan, we took a deep breath and traveled home to South Africa for a visit. We were nervous about how it would go. There was still lingering embarrassment from our abrupt departure. But we had a secret. It warmed us from the inside and carried us boldly forward. I was pregnant.

And with each roll of this baby's new body, each tap of his tiny feet on my belly, I felt God's Spirit whispering comfort and the fulfillment of promise in my heart. A Michigan baby headed to South Africa for the first time. We weren't returning empty handed. And one afternoon, crowded into my dad's sonogram room in the same building he'd worked at on Schoeman Street since the days I used to play receptionist at his office, Jackson and Karabo sat at the foot of the exam bed and jostled for a better view of the new baby.

We all watched Dad wave that small wand over my belly, muttering prayers for a clear picture of his new grandchild. We had one shot while we were home for him to be the one to find out if we were having a boy or a girl. With my heart in my throat, I watched as the same hands that had told me I was in labor with my firstborn prayed over the belly of my second. And I love to tell Micah the story of what happened when his oupa got the first glimpse of his tell-tale manhood—how he whooped with delight and yelled, "Thank you, Jesus!" And we all laughed till we cried at the joy of new beginnings right there in the ashes of the old ones.

The trip was full of understanding and friendship and family ties, tight and strong. Like fresh rain, it washed away the dirt and exhaustion of the last time we had been home. And we were left with clean memories. Ready for the imprint of new stories, fresh footprints. Then, after three weeks, we left. Again. And this time it hurt only in the good way.

On takeoff, a small foot added its own gum-boot beat to the ride. And a name flashed across my mind.

Micah.

We knew no one by that name. We knew very little about the book. Micah was a minor prophet, and his message included in the Bible is just a few short chapters long. When we got home, we looked it up and started to read. And over the echoes of the past two years of bumping up against so many noes, we heard whispers of a new yes.

But as for me, I will look to the LORD,
    I will wait for the God of my salvation;
    my God will hear me.

Rejoice not over me, O my enemy;
    when I fall, I shall rise;
when I sit in darkness,
    the LORD will be a light to me.
I will bear the indignation of the LORD
    because I have sinned against him,
until he pleads my cause
    and executes judgment for me.
He will bring me forth to the light;
    I shall behold his deliverance.

MICAH 7:7-9 (RSV)

God was speaking to us in new ways using the ancient words of a prophet to explain where we had come from and where we were going.

• • •

That was the year we invited everyone to our house for Christmas Eve. Pete's Grandpa and Grandma Hamilton were visiting from Florida. Aunt Marcia and Uncle David and their three kids were over, of course. Uncle Rod and Aunt Kim had come from Detroit with Ethan, Katie, and Sheldon. Pete's parents were in town. And on Christmas Eve they all cooked. We had ham, cheese balls and crackers, the famous twelve-layer Jell-O, and green bean casserole—food covering every countertop and snow falling on everything outside. We had a fireplace and a Christmas tree, with the decorations we'd collected from all the places we'd lived and visited in the last nearly decade, including the three angels that had once kept watch over Jackson's changing table.

My belly was stretched as taut and full as my heart. These people had brought home back to us. And embracing my South African tradition, they were holding printouts of the Nativity story, willing to each read a part like my family would be doing across the sea, under a hot Southern Cross sky.

Houses are made for people, not the other way around. That house, with its rows of pine trees marking the patchwork corners of Lakeside Drive and North Chipman Street that stitched together miles of cornfields, was our green pasture. It was our still waters, and the Lord led us gently beside and laid us down in peace, and on Christmas Eve we walked a path of faith that felt solid as sight. Grandma and Grandpa Hamilton read those long-ago verses of deliverance next to Uncle Rod, who never comes for a visit without bringing a massive pot of something delicious. Ethan and Jon pointed out that I'd missed one of them in designating the verses, and we scrambled to scratch out in pen new sections of the reading so there was a part for every cousin.

Uncle David had brought a snow globe bigger than Jackson's head, and that was the year Peter gave his teenage cousin Hans an album by Hans's favorite pop crush, and we all laughed so hard it was good medicine. The house that wasn't ours wrapped arms around us all, and we filled up every space in its kitchen built for big families with memories and photos. There was one especially of Grandma Hamilton sitting surrounded by her three daughters—the foundation stones of this oh-so-American, Midwest, Detroit Lions–loving family—on our red futon in the corner of the kitchen, in front of the window with its panorama of snow-piled countryside. I can close my eyes and see the scene right now. How they all grinned, perching on the too-small futon with its baby stains and battered sides.

Family. The DNA of my little Michigander who would be born just two days later.

WITH EACH NEW BABY,
we are that much more
vulnerable to having our
hearts broken into tiny
little bits of forever.

CHAPTER 9

there's nothing routine about the routine

THE FIRST TIME I gave birth, I wasn't afraid. I was in South Africa, home after a decade away, and poised on the edge of the vast unknown of childbirth, too inexperienced to know better. The second time I gave birth, fear wound its way into the picture. Because this time I knew what lay ahead; I had learned that pregnancy, like marriage, is an act of courage and faith. Every second-time mother knows the intimate joy of holding in her arms a being whose life is so new, so delicate that his skin is still translucent with heaven. She knows the smell of baby breath and the warmth of a heart that is beating with all four chambers for the first time. She knows.

But she also remembers. She remembers the hard work of

growing, carrying, and delivering that child into the world. She bears scars. And she needs to gird her courage around her to do it again. Death and life. Ask any pregnant mother, and you will find her thoughts equally consumed by both. Birth is hard and risky work. It is intimate and exposed at the same time. And the God born in a barn to a teenager and her novice husband can likely perfectly relate.

My water broke with Micah at two in the morning, just hours after Peter's parents had packed up their car and headed back to Illinois after spending Christmas with us. My water broke, but my contractions didn't start, and while in retrospect I wish I'd gone back to sleep for a few hours, I called the hospital and then Aunt Marcia instead. As soon as she and her girl, Cora, arrived with delight in their eyes, we handed the sleeping Jackson into their care and headed out into the snow.

In late December, every wintry Michigan breath exhales snow. The country road was quiet, velveted in white, and I felt a flutter of scared excitement run like goose bumps across my skin and settle a bit like nausea at the back of my throat. North Chipman is a long, winding road, and Peter drove it slowly through the thick flakes, his eyes wide with care, watching for deer.

My arrival was anticlimactic because labor hadn't started yet, but with the weather and my water having broken, they wanted me to stay at the hospital. So Pete and I walked long hallways and waited for the main event. And when it kicked in, I recognized it, like a familiar, ruthless friend, and I let it pummel away at me as hard and as long as I could before I reached the bridge of no going back and knew it was time to ask for the blessed epidural.

I held still through wave after wave of crashing contractions until my back was punctured and the relief slowly dripped through my body. I knew I'd pushed right up against the boundary line of what I could take and almost a step too far over it. But we had made it in time, and I could breathe again, and for forty-five minutes, it felt like the last time— two years and one country ago.

The anesthesiologist had been called away to an emergency C-section, and I was progressing quickly when I suddenly exploded out of the quiet calm of the epidural and into a wild, raging sea of advanced labor that took my breath away. I held on to the bed rail, looking wild eyed at Pete, and they paged another on-call anesthesiologist who lumbered in and tried to supplement the dose I'd been given. But the waves kept crashing, and it was only the next afternoon that I would find out I should have been given a much higher dose—that the epidural should have kept feeding medicine into my back until my lower half went quietly back to sleep. But I didn't know and the epidural didn't work, and I was alone and adrift on the open ocean. And I was terrified.

I had become a small ball of focus. I was disappearing under a heaving sea that I wasn't mentally prepared for, and I could feel myself drowning. I was certain I couldn't do it. I wanted out. I wanted out of my body, out of that room, out of the responsibility of wrestling a human being out of my insides. I turned my face into the cold metal of the delivery bed and let the tears come quietly, heavily down my cheeks. My hands gripped that side rail like it was my lifeline while my belly took on a life of its own.

I was the center of a bull's-eye, and I heard the one ruthless truth of motherhood pounding the inside of my eyelids. *The only way through is through. The only way through is through.* The terror tasted like metal in my mouth, and I couldn't swallow. Then a nurse came into the room, and she was as old as my mother would have been. She held my hand, spoke with authority, and told me that there was something I could do to feel better but that I wasn't going to like it. I grabbed at her. My face, my attention, my focus locked with hers as she told me to stop fighting the contractions but to push with them, to push through them, if I wanted relief.

And I believed her. I looked deep into her eyes full of the memories of a thousand women laboring hard over their children, and I pushed. Peter was an active participant this time, holding up one knee while my nurse, my believer, held up the other. And finally Dr. Chavez arrived, and for all his testosterone, he was full of tender experience and encouragement.

We were a team that rode the storm of labor together. They helped me believe that I could do it—that I could run this merciless marathon up and over the top of Everest one push, one desperate contraction at a time.

But Micah, like his brother before him, came at the wrong angle down the birth canal, his head stuck sideways, and no matter what I did or how hard I pushed, there was no budging him. It became a tug-of-war, with a suction cup attached to my Micah's head, and I was losing. For every centimeter he moved forward, he slipped back two. My leg muscles were shaking in the hands of my husband and my nurse.

"No," I told them. "Dr. Chavez, I can't. This baby isn't coming." I didn't believe he would ever be delivered, and I needed it to be over. I needed it to stop. I needed escape. And when I was giving up and trying to find a way out of myself, I will never forget how Dr. Chavez pulled himself up from between my legs until his face was level with mine and spoke directly into my eyes: "You are doing it. *You're* doing it." And wildly, I believed him.

But I needed eyes to go with my faith, and I gabbled to the room, "Can anyone see him? Can anyone see anything?" Dr. Chavez called for a mirror, and finally there—*there!*—was a small, dark head. And with that sight, unexpected reserves of courage cracked wide open in me, and I bore down and groaned what felt like my whole life out of myself for this new life. My world was one small head of hair, and my doctor removed himself and his round, rolling stool out of the way, hands raised in surrender, voice echoing in my ears: "You're doing it. *You're* doing it!" as I miraculously crossed the finish line and Micah's head came free. And Dr. Chavez was back cupping his hands to catch the rest of my second-born son as he emerged, finally, into a wintry Michigan afternoon.

Everyone was elated except me—I was too spent to celebrate. But they laid Micah gently on my chest, and I looked down at the face of the boy who had fought this battle with me. The boy whose name means "Who is like God?" Our gift for Christmas and a life restored. And there was Aunt Marcia taking his first photos, crying with us, watching Micah hold the finger of his father with a strong, mottled grip. And then they cut his cord, took his footprints, wrapped his body, and covered his head with a red-and-white cap. Micah was being warmed, and I was alone with my body that didn't remember how to stand.

My life has been littered with men who've said over and over again some variation of the same refrain: "I'm so glad I don't have to give birth. I could never do that." And maybe they're right. Birth costs. The act of giving life bleeds life from the giver. It's so hard that just standing up again afterward can take one's breath away. I couldn't have done it by myself. But there were the strong hands of a woman I'd never met at my side—a nurse who led me to a small bathroom after it was all over and turned on the shower. And when I couldn't stand by myself, couldn't stop my legs from shaking, couldn't find my center, she held me. She held me under the water, and I rested my forehead against the cold tile wall as the sweat and the blood from the battle washed away in warm rivulets at my feet.

And that night, when Peter wrote the rest of the family to tell them Micah had arrived safely, all eight pounds, five ounces of him, his e-mail began with these words: "Today, my courageous wife . . ."

• • •

Motherhood starts with such a bang—so many visitors, all that roar of adrenaline—that what comes next can be disorienting. Because after the high of childbirth comes a sleepless cycle of days that all run into one long, messy, nondescript blur. If there's one thing that can defeat a mother, it's the monotony. Get up, feed the baby, wash the laundry, change the diapers, do the dishes, make the car pool run, wrestle the math homework, figure out a new way to make chicken, change the sheets—times 365 days in a row. It's hard to see the significance when you're so weighed down by the mundane. And it can feel like everyone else around you is busy doing big, important things while you have worn the same spit-up-stained sweatpants three days in a row. You dread the "So what did you do today?" question as you rack your brain to come up with more than, "Cleaned up after the kids."

Some days the kids and I would all get dressed. But more often than not, we lived through that Michigan winter in our pajamas, hibernating in the back bedroom of a big house on a short country road. Pete was in the thick of the last months working on his dissertation while also juggling a job, so Micah and I camped out in the bed by ourselves while his dad pulled his own all-nighters upstairs.

Every morning Jackson would arrive in our room surprised to discover Micah was still around. "Micah's still here!" he'd announce in amazed tones, and we'd live our own version of *Groundhog Day* all over again. The days I got both boys dressed and into the car and down the long, snowy back roads to Meijer, the mega–grocery store, for a brief outing and then returned everyone in time for naps and meals and multiple diaper changes I counted as very full days.

I don't remember "doing" anything specific that winter. I'd rock Micah through the night shift with the radio playing the same songs I'd first heard when I was pregnant with Jackson in South Africa. "Blessed Be the Name of the Lord" fell over the room as the snow came down outside and I kick-pushed the chair back and forth with Micah curled up like a last rib against my chest. Peter and Jackson had put the rocking chair together while I was out one day before Micah arrived. With dutifully researched softness, yellow pillows, and white frame, it became our quiet corner cathedral as the radio played and I whispered old, familiar worship songs over Micah's future, my younger brother's upcoming marriage, Peter's job search.

In the morning I would try to entertain Jackson through Micah's long stretches of nursing and unpredictable naps. It was a season of slow—Pete traveling for work, the world asleep as far as I could see from the kitchen windows. Knee-high drifts of white were pockmarked by the occasional wild turkey or deer. Sunshine would make it through some days and stream through the windows, warming the cherry reds in the wood floors. Jackson would play with his paints or his new toy kitchen, and Micah would be either in my arms or in the bouncy, car-shaped ExerSaucer we'd scored at a consignment sale downtown when my mother-in-law was up visiting one weekend.

Aunt Marcia would often come over after work just to hold the baby. She'd blow in with tight hugs, shedding shoes and coat and pieces of her day at the door and sit on the futon to cradle Micah with her arms and me with her presence. With my liberated hands, I'd cook dinner, wash dishes, pick up toys. She'd always bring her daughter. Cora and Jackson would run laps in the basement with its deep, thick carpet we didn't have enough furniture to fill. From my perch at the stove, I could hear him screaming with laughter. Sometimes Cora and her little brother, Jon, would get him all dressed up and out into the snow to toddle tracks, face-plant, and then come back in for hot chocolate. Spring was slow coming in Michigan, but we weren't in a hurry.

Some days my head would pound and I'd wonder how to tug-of-war my way forward at the pace of both a toddler and a newborn. For a while I tried to figure out how to cook. I was enamored of the idea of sneaking healthy substitutes into my kids' food and tried to buy every vegetable necessary for an entire cookbook of purees in a single outing. I got maybe two batches in before everything went bad and I resigned myself to mac and cheese from a box without a boost of squash.

Winter finally melted into spring, and in my memory that spring will always be defined by birdseed. We had several bird feeders you could see from the kitchen windows, and when May arrived, the seed that had spilled from them sprouted in the grass below and grew wild and enthusiastic— a sort of knockoff corn that it never occurred to us to trim or pull. Jackson would let the seeds run through his fingers as we refilled the containers that smelled so sweet of cedar, and we never came up with a successful way to keep the squirrels out of them.

On our quietest, least interesting days, I got better at hearing the music of motherhood. Because I know what typically plays in the background is the chaos of squabbles and coats never put away in the right place or muddy boot tracks across the carpet. There are the to-do lists that never get done because the baby has croup and you're up with him all night for a week praying that the warm steam from a shower you let run for more than an hour at 1 a.m. will help him breathe easily enough to nurse again. And still your three-year-old needs to eat, and there's no sleeping in for moms and no escaping the fact that today might be the day you lose at laundry roulette because this time there really are no more pairs of clean underwear buried in the pile at the foot of the dryer that everyone's been rooting around in for a week.

In the dark and the tired and the everydayness of those moments, I started to feel it—the weight of glory, the glorious ordinary that is a gift to us who are knee deep in a world where it can sometimes feel like we have lost all the parts of ourselves we used to know like the back of our hands, our favorite jeans, our own names. A gift from a God who names every part of who we are and what we do significant. Because "he is before all things, and in him *all things hold together*."[1] There is no part of our everyday, wash-and-repeat routine of kids and laundry and life and fights and worries and playdates and aching budgets and preschool orientations and work and marriage and love and new life and bedtime marathons that Jesus doesn't look deep into and say, "That is Mine."

In Him *all* things hold together.

Every day I would walk to the mailbox with Jackson, and every day I'd try to convince him that we didn't need to walk up the street to wave at the neighbor who was sometimes outside on his riding mower. Every day he'd set his chin and turn his back to me and take off for the end of the street anyway. I would notice the fallen pine needles, how they crunched under our feet, and the evergreen branches above, how they caught the light, fanning out in shades of dark and honey. Jackson would wave and I'd make the same conversation as yesterday, and neither of us could hear ourselves over the engine. But there was fellowship in the waving, nodding, grinning three-year-old.

Aunt Marcia introduced us to their babysitter, Helen, who was like the sixth member of their family, and she added her lessons to all the others—how to be patient, how to generously bless, how to look life in the eye, undaunted, and how to always open your arms to one more baby. And there was one perfect day when I got Jackson to eat tomato soup. His eyes were massive below his summer's buzz cut, and he stood bare chested at the kitchen counter launching spoonful after spoonful into his mouth, declaring, "Soupa!" as we both laughed and the long, fading light of afternoon colored the room.

Slowly, being a mother became more than a series of moments connected only by dirty diapers, empty baby wipe bins, toy cars strewn all over the bathroom floor, and bum cream. There was a harmony rising from the eclectic collection of tasks every mother cycles through in a day—this sacred marriage of the mundane and the eternal. The small directly related to the massive; kids walking around like so much eternity with skin on.

Pete and I would sit out on the back deck at night and watch fireflies. Some weekends friends from Chicago would sit with us. Friends who knew our story and most of its layers. Church was still a constant, and we hosted home group at our house every week. The house was meant for many more people than just us four. The lawn needed scads of kids to appreciate all its wide-open room for running at breakneck, helter-skelter speeds just because. Micah would be passed from lap to lap until he got too tired and ornery to be cute anymore, and I'd tuck him into the white crib we got at consignment and go back to my paper-plate helping of barbecue meatballs.

We bought a small pop-up canopy from Walmart and a set of lawn furniture. I hung pots of flowers from each corner, and one day that summer Grandpa Doehring sat out on the deck for six hours watching his grandkids and great-grandkids and telling us all over and over again, "This is life." Uncle David had brought over their lawn chairs on the back of the old red pickup so we'd have enough seats to go around for the two sets of grandparents, one set of parents, brothers, sisters-in-law, cousins, aunts, uncles, and kids. Jackson wore blue overalls and red sandals, and that was the summer his hair was white blond and we spent more time with Pete's family than we had in the previous decade. Norman Rockwell collided with Tom Sawyer that June, and I always remember those two years in Michigan as a tapestry, with Micah tightly woven into the fabric.

The house on the corner of North Chipman Street was our refuge and that row of pine trees our hedge of protection, and it was a time out of time for rediscovering that everything can be made new. Especially the parts we thought were cracked, chipped, broken forever. A steam train bellowed from the tracks that passed a mile or so away, and John Deere combines combed through the fields along M-52. Peter traveled a lot for work, and I traveled deeper into the rhythms of discovering the world behind the eyes of my small people. Work filtered into the picture for me, too. I taught at the community college and worked as a research consultant.

But I remember juggling jobs like a hazy filter over a much brighter photograph. The four of us discovering that two kids are much more than one, and my seeing my husband through hardworking Michigan eyes—a man who provides for his people. And one afternoon in a sandwich shop tacked onto Walmart, we cried over a phone call that offered him the job that made sense of our story, and we hugged each other with more relief and joy than the day two months earlier when he'd walked across the stage and finally received his PhD.

• • •

It had rained every time we'd moved. Every. Single. Time. So when we threw a pizza party for anyone willing to help us pack up Michigan for our move to Virginia, I wasn't surprised at all when once all the pizza had been eaten and the kids were sprawled in exhausted heaps all over the yard and the parents finally turned skeptical attention to our mountains of boxes, the clouds started to roll in.

Everyone had come out. Our church and home group and community friends. The house stretched and spilled over with people and two years' worth of starting over. We'd boxed up everything. Pete's mom had been in town and had given us a head start, packing the entire kitchen while Micah puked round after round of stomach bug and Jackson played with the packing paper. I duct-taped bags of flour and rice and beans closed until the house was more storage than seating and we were ready.

Bets were made as to whether or not the U-Haul we'd rented would be able to absorb all the contents of the house, but the men were committed to helping Pete make it happen. Aunt Marcia took the boys back to her place, and the packing began in earnest, each box full of more life than we ever could have imagined hauling away from this season that had started with so many layers of no. My hands were sticky with packing tape and my back hurt, but each box loaded, each counter wiped down, each room vacuumed was a benediction of grace, of thanks, of promises and mercies that are new every morning.

And when the rain came, the teenagers took up the dare and rushed the back of the truck with the last remnants of our Michigan lives until we were all laughing—a crazy packing rain dance of good-bye to what had been one of my favorite beginnings. The ramp got slippery, the truck bulged, and when it came to choosing between the futon and the toy train table, I stepped over the dividing line squarely into life as a mom first when we rammed that inherited play table between the last unpacked cracks and slid down the door and locked up our journey and our memories. And the house that had welcomed us exhaled and released us back into the real world.

Pete drove the truck while I flew with the boys, and we landed back in Washington, DC, where it had all started two kids, three continents, and a decade earlier. There was a small, white rental house waiting for us in northern Virginia with enough of a backyard for the boys to dig up and doom me to a continual state of embarrassed acquiescence. The tree in front stood sentinel-like, one massive branch raised in a perpetual salute of welcome. That first night the only things we unpacked were the beds. And when the boys were asleep, Pete and I sat in a sea of boxes and looked back across eleven years together.

Eleven years of a routine I knew by heart—I could do every step, every move with both eyes closed. Our glasses and piles of favorite books on the nightstands. The smell of Polo cologne. Bath times and bedtimes, Spider-Man toothpaste and Superman body wash. A hundred hundred glasses of water after lights-out. Playdates and lunches, school applications and toy tractors. Two-stepping through the kitchen and through temper tantrums, over the laundry and past the rows of photos framing the rhyme, the rhythm of this last decade. In sync. Swaying to the tired and the life crammed into the weekend and the preparation for Mondays, to the orchestra of a family that sings off-key and with abandon. A crescendo of beautiful chaos in the living room between the two couches that came back with us from South Africa, with the toy tiger sprawled at our feet.

And the dance swept on.

My hand still in his, even on the nights when I beat his chest and asked all the whys that have no answer and lay in the dark and listened to us both breathing, as we have since our first dance accompanied by wedding rings.

I was already starting to love the melody we were making together in this new house that Jackson wished had stairs. It sounded like a boy's pat on his brother's back. Like LEGOs that spill out of toy boxes and hushed moments under the night sky for last stories, boys' plots, secrets between the top and bottom bunks. Like sand, gritty against my toes where it had escaped socks and sandboxes and taken up residence at the foot of my bed. Like the hushed quiet of Sunday afternoon naps, complete with the creased faces that emerge from under the covers for hot tea and cookies. And like fart jokes. Lots and lots of fart jokes.

Motherhood is
a sacred marriage of
the mundane and
the eternal.

how to fall
in like

I WASN'T WHAT my mother-in-law expected. A tall South African girl who spirited her son away after his senior year of college to another state and then to another country—several other countries, actually. I must have taken some getting used to—not to mention the obscenely high phone bills. She's quiet where I am loud. Thoughtful where I am wordy. Deliberate where I am impulsive. Short where I am tall. Yet my mother-in-law has grown into my mother over these last nearly two decades. She is now my first phone call, and her second name, like mine, is Jo.

It took some prying at the hinges to find a way to creak open the everyday ins and outs of having a mother again. I live an ocean away from my father. It had been a long time since I was daily accountable to any kind of parent—it's surprisingly easy to slip out of the habit.

I've heard tell about daughters who sweat days ahead of time to get their house shipshape for a mother-in-law's visit. Instead, I make lists of chores she has offered to help me with. The house bleeds laundry, and I know when she gets here, things will be better. She cleans the insides of my fridge and packs up boxes of clothes that should have been donated the last time we moved. She researches whether the garbage collectors will pick up expired paint or if we need to drop it at a special location. She loves us with busy hands and tireless tasks checked off the list.

And when she's not in my house—when she's back in Illinois and I'm here—I know she's praying. She learned it from her own mother. The faithful prayers of a woman who isn't just being polite when she says, "I'll pray for you." I've come to recognize that for her, that phrase isn't the worn-out cliché I'm used to, but the battle cry of a warrior. I don't take it for granted anymore. And as I go deeper into the territory of parenting Micah, I hold on to it like a lifeline.

Micah was eight months old when we moved to Virginia. Ever since he was born, it seems, he has loved me with the intensity of a cannibal. He ate up my time, my patience, my personal space, and my temper. His first two years were so intense I felt like I was trying to breathe underwater. He was my shadow, my watchman, my second skin. There was no me and Micah. There was only Micah. Every morning he woke up early and came into bed with Pete and me, but he wasn't interested in Pete. It was me he wanted. Me he wanted to pretzel with—our limbs all entwined and his chubby face mashed down on my cheek, his breathing raspy in my ear.

Painful morning after morning, I learned that it was futile to try to shift him. To try to reset the angle of my elbow or shoulder so I had more room than your average circus contortionist in a cube would have been a lost cause. There was no moving; there was only acquiescence. He must have me and I must let him, or his internal fire alarm would go off for hours. I learned to lie still and surrender my mornings to this boy who was so desperately hungry for his mother. And I had to eat my own words—how I had often scoffed at the idea of the "strong-willed child." So ignorant and arrogant. Experience has been humbling.

I entered a new world with Micah—an extreme kind of parenting that made me dizzy and light headed with the lack of personal space. Because the more I gave him, the more he needed. His ferocious love was almost impossible to satisfy. His appetite for almost everything wildly outstripped his big brother's. Where Jackson picked at his food, Micah inhaled it. Where Jackson hugged, Micah lunged. As a baby, Micah blew through milk and formula and quickly moved on to solids and steaks and mashed potatoes. If he could gum it, he would eat it.

He wailed through every day care and preschool parting. And I ached the wretched separation, yet when I came to pick him up each day, he was grinning and I could have cried again—this time from the relief of hearing the stories about how well he had done, about the cardboard crocodile he'd made, about the toy workbench he loved, about the friends he hugged individually at every good-bye. But on Sundays, when he was supposed to be in Sunday school, he clung and wept, and while the well-meaning teachers told me he would eventually cry it out, I explained to them that even toddlers are entitled to a Sabbath. To a rest.

So I stood in church on Sunday mornings, my arms full of a boy who didn't realize that he was no longer a baby. Two and a half, and I was still moved by his stubborn insistence that he and I were one heart beating in two (barely) separate bodies.

But I felt the worship in ways I didn't when those same arms were empty.

The top of his head fit perfectly underneath my chin, and with one hand he clutched his baby bear, and with the other he oh-so-softly patted my back, right at the top of my shoulder blades.

I rocked him and sang praise for his Maker into an ear hidden behind soft curls that brushed my top lip and tickled my nose. And suddenly, suddenly, all those great and powerful phrases like "sacrifice" and "loves like a hurricane" and "blessed be the name of the Lord" took on Technicolor meaning.

With this boy wrapped in my arms, this flesh and blood and bone that I had grown in my womb, clinging to me, I understood what the God parent feels for me. To die for this love—yes, it made sense.

I sang and I ached, and I knew that He loves me like this. This wrenching and tugging at the gut as we rocked and the drums beat and the worship invited us to sing away our fear, our failures, our despair. I was Micah and Micah was me in that moment, and the music wrapped up and around us until my head flooded with the knowledge that this was how I was held. This was how.

And to do this, the heavenly Father had to unwrap His arms from around His only Son. Unmake the closeness. Break more than the ties of flesh and blood. And heaven itself cracked open when He let go of His Son and reached for me.

I stood. I stood in the worship with one arm cupped around my boy and the other reaching up and out to the God who had given him to me. Desperate not to disappoint. Desperate to catch hold of the hand He offered. Desperate to whisper my thanks. In the music, in the small words, in the rocking of the baby who was becoming a boy, I poured out my gratitude.

And my arms—how they ached with the weight of it.

• • •

Pete and I parented on and discovered that life with two boys can be wildly unpredictable. So I wasn't surprised one day when Peter muttered, "We're never buying anything nice until the boys are in college," because frankly the destruction level between the two of them must be given its due respect.

They share a bedroom, and threatening to separate them

if the noise level doesn't go down to a whisper after lights-out is the ultimate punishment. They thrive on each other. And they inspire each other to impressive acts of childhood idiocy. One night I discovered Micah hanging from the outside of his crib. His feet were precariously balanced on a wildly wobbling Diaper Genie trash can that Jackson had dragged into place in an attempt to Houdini him free. And when I confronted them with a gaping jaw and a gasped, "You guys are so naughty!" Jackson defiantly and infamously responded with arms set akimbo on his tiny hips and eyes looking straight back at mine, "Mama, we're not naughty. We're brothers!"

This was the logic that colored my days and nights, and in between I commuted interminable hours between preschool and work and my own worries for my kids, and all the while my second born continued to give me stretch marks long after he'd made it out of the womb.

When Micah was three, Pete's dad came out for a visit, and we spent a terrible afternoon in Annapolis. Our second son was as stormy as the skies above the Naval Academy in late October, and it was hopeless—all my hissing and threatening and dragging him along, hoping for the miracle of obedience. Or at the very least enjoyment in the outing. Instead, we simply crashed over and over again into the stubborn set of his mouth and his ferociously crossed arms—his refusal to comply, to eat his hot dog, to stay seated, to keep out of the road, to walk with us, to sit inside his stroller. At one point he sat down in the middle of a crowded sidewalk and screamed, and all the tourists weaving their way between the tightly packed stores selling T-shirts and ice cream, wooden carvings of various famous lakes and Navy gear scowled at me and glanced sympathetically at him. We hadn't even begun the tour of campus yet.

By the end of the day, I was dripping sweat on the outside and swear words on the inside. My head was pounding from balancing the expectations of the day with the reality of my son. And that night, as we all sat exhausted around the kitchen table, Pete's dad said what I'd known he was thinking all along. To be fair, he only put into words what I'd been thinking myself: "I would have spanked that kid on about three separate occasions today."

And I was so desperate because as much as I would have liked to, as much as some might say it would have helped, three years with Micah had taught me better. I'd learned the lay of the land and that roughness or temper from me was like gasoline on the fire that burns deep and wild in Micah's gut. I know at some instinctual level that I can't put into words that I need to lead him out from under this desperate burden of temper tenderly. But I can't see the path, and sometimes I fear we're both lost deep in the dark.

It was at this breaking point, when I was reeling from raising a son with a temper that far outstrips my own, that I called my mother-in-law to warn her of the report she would surely hear about my failed parenting. Because when someone has washed your kids' dirty underwear, it becomes easier to share the other dirty secrets that won't come clean through pure force of will or bleach. I tucked the phone under my ear and whispered the fears no mother wants to say out loud. About how I just couldn't make sense of this one, couldn't figure out how to calm or raise or love him so that his rage wouldn't get in the way of our family. And how he seemed as desperate as I was to be rid of his temper but remained trapped nonetheless—tear streaked, red faced, and lisping words out of a deep well of despair: "Mama, I don't know how to make it stop."

Being a practical woman of God, Debbie was already looking for the next step. Prayer, yes. But how to pray? Where to direct our words? Who to request backup from? She reminded me that children are born of the Spirit as much as of their parents' DNA, and perhaps that's where we should focus. I was so tired. I knew the next battle round with Micah would come at breakfast when he got the wrong color bowl or there wasn't enough milk on his cereal or the spoon I gave him was the wrong size. I already knew I wouldn't have the energy for it. So she promised to pray with me. She offered Tuesdays—suggested that we fast and pray together every week so that even though we weren't together, I wouldn't feel alone.

It has been a lifeline. I hold on with both hands. The rock and roll of the days lessens, and I think I can do this. It's still hard, but it's no longer lonely. Women see children with different eyes than husbands do. I know she sees Micah and she sees me, and there is a solution to this puzzle if I can just see a new way to parent my passionate second born.

His fervor is a good thing—I know this. But his rage takes all the potential of his beautiful passion and tears it into tiny bits like so many shredded pieces of the painting he tore up one night before dinner. He loves to paint. He loves the textures, the water, the colors, choosing the paper. So he spent time and poured his imagination into all that wet collage of color. But when he compared it to what his brother was doing, when there was even a hint of criticism and when a long day was added to a short fuse, he burst into a fiery baby iconoclast. And once he'd torn the paper in half, he collapsed into a small version of himself and cupped dimpled hands around his short, tender hair and cried like he'd lost his best friend.

A year earlier, my mother-in-law had spotted the squint in Jackson's eye that I'd missed for months. In a lifetime of elementary school teaching, she'd spent her days looking into the eyes of children, and she said he needed to go to the optometrist. I'd just thought he needed a time-out for his annoying habit of ignoring the toys right in front of his feet when he'd been asked to pick them up. So I took him, but the pediatrician didn't find anything out of the ordinary.

"Take him somewhere else," she insisted.

And while normally I would have been too tired to try again, she was there at the time, washing and folding the clothes, apparently unfazed by the chaos and the things that never get done in our small rental house, so I asked for a referral and made an appointment with the pediatric ophthalmologist.

She was back in Illinois when I called with the news that she'd been right—a terribly lazy eye and severe astigmatism. A problem that, uncorrected, could have caused permanent damage. He ended up with blue SpongeBob glasses. So when I couldn't see Micah properly, I knew where to go.

Debbie and I traced family trees and genes and remembered that blue eyes aren't the only traits children inherit by blood. I stopped being defeated by Micah and instead started to research him. I studied my son. And God started to show me how to see. Not with a magnifying glass, but with a mirror. I saw my own temper. I saw generations of temper before that. Sometimes you don't realize you have a temper until you have kids. And then one night someone carves a pattern into the leather sofa. Or someone dumps the messy contents of a pencil sharpener all over the floor after you've told him not to touch it. Or someone gets out of bed for the ten thousandth time, when you've finally sat down and there's only an hour left before sleep slams into your eyelids.

There's no rage like the exhausted rage of motherhood.

These are the things they don't talk about in the parenting books or playgroups or coffee dates. How you will one day lose your ever-loving mind because two boys peed all over the bathroom shelf just to see what kind of range they could get. This on an evening after I'd kept my temper all day against the onslaught of Micah's. When I'd given grace after he'd yelled that he was running away and started off down the block with face red and furious. When I'd chased after him, preaching that people don't leave this family. When I'd loved and patiently intervened one hundred different times after he'd gotten angry in one hundred different ways that others were sucking up the time and attention he wanted, needed, demanded.

Some days you've done it right—you've been reasonable in the face of irrational toddlerhood and you've bent low to meet the needs of tiny humans straining against their own limitations. You've reminded yourself that you're the grown-up, and you've tried really hard to act like it.

Some days you get it right, right up to the finish line.

And then your kids soak the bathroom floor, shelf, and mirror in their newfound manhood. Or a son flings his toothbrush, dunks his head in the bathwater after he's already in pajamas, refuses to quit asking for that one last snack—and it's easy to let the temper pour out of you like a hot rush of lava. And it can feel so good. With clenched fists and jaw and gut, you have a wild meltdown easily as irrational as your kids'.

These are the ragged fringes of motherhood that don't make for pretty pictures. These are the moments that no one teaches you about in the breast-feeding classes or includes with the instructions for putting the baby to bed on his back or thinks to write on a warning label. This guarantee that kids will push your buttons and their boundaries, and there will be an afternoon when it is almost impossible to remember that you are the parent and that you can't parent effectively with an out-of-control temper.

So I started to pay attention to my own anger. I saw how

lazy my prayers were, how haphazard my approach to helping Micah control his own anger. How my parenting had
mostly been a mixture of embarrassment and frustration.

I saw how long it had been since I'd enjoyed him.

And I began to exercise my motherhood again. I stretched
and bent and prayed. I fasted and paid attention and listened.
I apologized and meant it. These words that can stick in the
throat of grown-ups but that are like sacred, unexpected treasure when you place them in the tiny hands of your children.

And instead of floundering in the stories everyone else
told me about him, I began to draft Micah's own narrative.
I wrote it down. Deliberately. How I wanted to see this son
of mine. How I wanted to teach others to see him.

I sent these words to his frustrated preschool teacher:

*We so appreciate your partnership. We value
Micah and the work that Christ is doing in his heart.
He is extremely sensitive to the stories of Jesus and
understands that his name means "Who is like God?"
and that his second name, Peter, means "the rock."
We are encouraging him to be a man who lives in the
blessing of his name and is a leader and an encourager
and a protector of others.*

I began to sense Micah growing in my heart with flutters
much like when I first felt him moving in my belly. I cradled
this new story. It was a relief to be writing it again and not
just turning the pages, terrified of what came next. I prayed

for him more in one month than perhaps all the rest of his months combined. I prayed, and praying was writing his story, and writing was realizing, and realizing was seeing. I saw glimpses of the story God has for my Micah. I spoke it out loud over him.

Sometimes, in the beginning, when I was still finding the words, I only prayed over him when he was asleep. I made his bed my prayer bench. And when he woke up and asked me what I was doing, I was too embarrassed to tell him.

"Mama, whatcha doin'?" he asked with words slurred by sleep.

I was crouched over the bottom bunk, his white Christmas lights strung about my head and his brother's top bunk. I started to make something up, to say I was just checking on him.

But then I caught myself, and I gave the truth to his sleep-groggy ears straight: "I am praying for you. I am praying that all your big, wild, strong feelings will make you a great warrior for God's Kingdom."

He yawned, whispered, "Okay," and rolled over.

As he slept, I stared at the back of his sleep-matted hair. I listened to him start to snore gently and counted the seven, eight, nine stuffed animals surrounding him. I wondered how he even fit into that bed with all the swords, eclectic collection of toy tools, and puppies clamoring for space alongside him. In that moment I caught something unexpected. My stomach ached with a tender *like* for this son of mine.

I liked that this was how he chose to sleep. I liked how his bedtime zoo so perfectly illustrated his compassion for all living things. I liked how his big, clumsy limbs that he was still growing into were draped diagonally across the bunk. I liked that the radio was on because he had been dancing for me just before going to bed. I liked how he slept in the same position as his dad and how he thrived on the same routine every night. I liked the glass of water he always asked for and kept close to his bed, just like me. I liked the discarded book on dinosaurs he was reading and the pen and notepad he always had under his pillow.

I liked that he and I were fighting on the same team and not against each other anymore. I liked that some days he would come and find me after an outburst and quietly whisper a new and powerful sentence, "I'm sorry for shouting, Mama."

I liked that he was learning to name his bad feelings, and we were together claiming all the power in his passion for something stronger than rage and braver than temper tantrums. I liked that we were writing the story together and that he was becoming the hero who held on to his temper with both hands and told me proudly how he'd done so.

I liked him so much I could hardly breathe. I just sat in that room between a toy tiger and a radio playing softly and stroked the sweaty forehead of a nearly four-year-old and let the like keep filling me up, all the way to overflowing.

• • •

When you haven't had a mother to go to for more than half your life, you have to relearn the instinct to bring her your sorrow, your petty worries, your dirty fridge. But when she meets you with grace, open arms, and tips for reconnecting with your son and cleaning the grout in your bathtub, you keep coming back.

When I had this book growing in my belly but no time to deliver it onto paper, I called her. Prayer partner, built-in encourager, she committed to be with me in spirit every 5 a.m. when I was dragging myself out from under the warm covers and into the quiet playroom to tap out my story, before I thought anyone would ever read it. I do not like early mornings. But I knew she would be up too, getting ready for school, waiting to hear from me about how the writing went. So I'd pull my crazed hair into a ponytail, slip on my glasses, and sit for a few uninterrupted hours of remembering the days I thought I never wanted to be anybody's mother.

I think of her every time I make tea. I used to think of my own mom, who loved tea so. But now I think of Debbie. It's funny how old memories can get wallpapered over with newer, fresher ones, and every time I look at the microwave with my mug in it, it's all Debbie.

It's faster to just nuke the hot water in our old microwave— the one with the slight crack running down the front door. When we lived in Michigan, the microwave was stored in the garage because the kitchen came with one built in. And when we came back from one of Micah's checkups, Debbie was driving because I was still recovering from my difficult delivery.

Micah had pounded his way into the world from the

get-go. Snow blanketed the tiny town of Owosso, and I was sitting at a strange angle in the passenger seat, trying to find the most comfortable position for my uncomfortable body, when she pulled in to the garage. I could tell there wasn't going to be enough room between the microwave and the car's front bumper. But I can still see her in the corner of my mind—so certain we'd make it and calmly not taking my advice and then tapping right into that plastic door.

That was before I could tease her like I do now about always being right. But now—now I can wrap my arms around her at Thanksgiving and chuckle and call her Mom, tease her about our differences, and not doubt for a single second that we are family or that when she prays, all heaven listens.

GOD STARTED TO SHOW ME
HOW TO SEE MY SON.

Not with a
magnifying glass,
but with a mirror.

when you're scared motherhood means missing out on your life

THERE WAS A Sunday after church when I so badly wanted to capture a family photo. We had very few of these. Primarily because the thought of wrangling my children and myself into decent clothes and attitudes simultaneously made me break out in full-body sweats. But a friend who's a professional photographer had offered to do a session for free, and it was enough to make Pete and me throw caution to the wind and begin planning how to trick our offspring into appearing camera friendly. There were definitely Wendy's chicken nuggets involved.

It was a warm fall day. Everyone was suitably attired,

and there was much false enthusiasm and excitement on the part of Pete and me. The boys seemed to be buying it. We'd brought a soccer ball, and they were kicking it around the grassy field in back of our church and allowing us to grab them, all grinning in the direction of the camera, during the breaks. But Micah wasn't feeling that great, and between fits of coughing, there was a moment when he looked like he was going to gag up the bottle of milk he'd put away. And I? I lunged at him, because the last thing I needed was that puke ending up on his fresh photo-shoot-ready shirt. So I instinctively did the unthinkable—I caught it in my hands. And wiped them off and told Mallory to keep shooting.

But the boys kept getting antsier and antsier, and I could feel the sweat running down my sides, and finally it was time to wave the white flag and head back to the car. We stopped at the stone benches before the parking lot to see if we could catch one more moment. I had on my grim mommy face—glaring at the boys to sit, to hold still, to please, just one more time, look at the camera, stop sticking out your tongue, and behave, for the love of all that is holy. *Just help me out.*

I could feel the rage rising in me. The frustration over not being able to control the picture frame—a constantly moving target with two sons under six. And before I knew it, Jackson was so over it, and he took off running toward the parking lot. I was just steps behind him, determined to rein him in—partly for his safety, but mostly out of determination not to have my son flaunt me so publicly, so blatantly. I reached out for his hoodie, but he skipped ahead of me. My fingers closed on air, my boots tripped out from under me, and there was nothing to break my fall. My chin hit the concrete first. I felt the impact ricochet through my entire body. I was sure my chin had been pushed backwards and up into my head. I couldn't move. I just turned my head slowly to the side so I could rest it against the cool sidewalk.

I'm not sure how long I lay there. Nausea came and went. My eyes burned, watering with the impact of the pain. I couldn't be touched. I couldn't stand. My head felt like shattered glass. And my jaw? I was terrified to touch my jaw. Terrified of what I might find. Picture perfect it was not. And even in that moment, I knew that every time I looked at that beautifully smiling family in the photo, this was the part I'd remember. How it came at the cost of so much sweat, puke, and crazy eyes on the part of the mother, who just wanted to fit in with all the other mothers smiling at her from the annual Christmas cards.

These are not the moments they tell you about when you're expecting.

How one day I would literally have to be peeled off the sidewalk because I lost my temper with a five-year-old and fell flat on my face. How when I was unsteady and my jaw was covered in black and blue, it wouldn't occur to me to get it checked out by a doctor because there were kids to get home and feed and a business trip to go on the next day. How I'd lost myself in the role of the professional juggler so deeply, so wholly, that I'd also lost all perspective.

• • •

Twenty-four hours later I was in the Pacific Northwest, one of only a handful of women at a conference for so-called emerging leaders. Most of the attendees and all the speakers were men. The only woman invited to take the stage was there to introduce her male mentor. But the pieces of her story we got as part of her introduction were powerful. Straight from college, she'd taken on the daunting job of bringing clean water to Africa with a brand-new NGO. Her story resonated powerfully with mine as I sat listening from a table close to the front. I hadn't grown up dreaming of being a mother. I'd grown up dreaming of being a human rights lawyer.

I was born into the heart of darkness, when apartheid in South Africa was at its peak, and I grew up watching its madness spin out of control. Literally translated "separation," apartheid meant that our schools were still segregated when I entered high school in 1987, and Nelson Mandela was well into his twenty years behind bars. And while I got to see that system crumble by my senior year and Nelson Mandela released from prison and eventually elected president in the first free election of our nation's history, those outrages were seared into my memory early.

I was fourteen when I felt it for the first time—the desperation in my bones to make things right. I was standing in our driveway with the bougainvillea spilling over the wall, listening to my mom tell me what had happened to our gardener, Piet. He traveled dirt roads between his various jobs, and walking was slow business—an effort he started before sunrise each day. So she studied with him and took him to get his driver's license, but after several unsuccessful attempts, it looked like he wouldn't be passing anytime soon. In the meantime, he needed a better way to get around, so she and my father had bought him a mountain bike. Piet had had it less than a month when my mom came home and punctured my world with her words.

"He was on his way home today when two guys in a bakkie drove him off the road," Mom said. "They wanted to know who he'd stolen the bike from."

I could feel my chest tighten.

"He told them we'd bought it for him. But they didn't believe him. Or at least they said they didn't. I don't think it would have mattered what he said."

"But why, Mom?"

"Because, my love, they wanted a fight more than they wanted the truth."

"I don't understand."

"Lisa-Jo, they had a sjambok with them."

That's when my face got gritty and the tears started to burn down my embarrassed cheeks. These men who shared my skin color and the language of half my family tree—they carried the stuff of children's nightmares and tall tales in the back of their pickup truck?

Grandpa Rous had a sjambok on the farm. He used to crack it from horseback over the heads of the sheep we were rounding up. My dad could crack it so loud it scared us kids.

It hung on a hook on the farmhouse wall. And in the hands of a sheep farmer, it was a tool.

But in the apartheid of my childhood, it was also a weapon, a cruel favorite, a curse.

"They whipped Piet and stole his bike. I took him to the hospital."

She was very still. I couldn't read her face. My nails were cutting lines on the insides of my clenched fists.

"But we have to go to the police! We need to report it, right?"

She just stood there, staring at me. I couldn't understand a word of what she wasn't saying.

"No," she said, like a shrug, like a sigh, like surrender. "It won't matter. They won't do anything."

And that's when I felt it—the desperation to change things. "We have to do *something*!" It came out like a childish whine. I thought I was going to throw up.

"Yes." And she just kept standing there in the sunshine, her glasses looking through me. "But to change things, you will have to change the law. You have to change the system from the inside." She said it like she was talking to herself, like she was looking back on her years working in a free advice clinic for domestic workers who were seeking proper pay or severance or leave from their indifferent employers.

But I heard it as my own battle cry, and I held on to it all through college and law school. But by the time I emerged with my degree, South Africa had turned a corner. A black president had been elected, his birthday had been declared a national holiday, the system had finally been gutted, and the process of painfully rebuilding the country from the inside had begun.

I watched in wonder from an ocean away and drifted with the rest of my law class into a big firm, surprised to find myself practicing corporate litigation in Chicago instead of human rights law in Africa. Then 9/11 happened. I was on the thirty-fifth floor of the Mercantile Exchange building, my window eye-to-eye with the Sears Tower. And while the rest of the building evacuated, a senior partner stood in my office giving instructions about a case, punctuating his insistence with his index finger as people streamed out of the office behind him.

By the end of that month, I'd quit my job and moved with Pete to Kyiv, Ukraine, where he'd been offered a national security fellowship. We planned to be there for ten months but ended up staying two and a half years. And it was in Ukraine that I learned what it feels like, what it takes, how it aches to be part of change from the inside out.

I'd heard about human trafficking, of course. But I hadn't seen it close-up. I didn't know what the faces of twenty-something girls look like when they return vacant and ashamed from what they'd thought would be an au pair job or a waitressing gig or a chance to support their families from abroad.

In our first month in Kyiv, I attended a conference on counter–human trafficking with Pete. I didn't have a job yet, so I decided to tag along with him to learn, to connect, to find something to keep me busy during his ten-month assignment.

The event was held in a huge, old ballroom with heavy brocade curtains. The tables were arranged in a massive horseshoe and covered with starched white cloths, and there were nameplates in letters I couldn't read yet. I sat in the second row of chairs arranged against the wall—an observer, not an expert. Representatives from organizations I'd never heard of shared their battle scars and platforms and strategies for fighting this scourge that had so badly battered and bruised Eastern Europe.

But it was the last speaker who 100 percent caught my attention and set my pulse pounding. He was the chief of mission for an organization that was part of the United Nations' country team in Ukraine. They were pursuing a threefold counter-trafficking program that included prevention and advocacy, prosecution and criminalization, and protection and reintegration. As part of their program, they had established a medical center solely dedicated to the mission of treating returning victims of trafficking. Doctors and psychologists devoted their time to rebuilding the broken stories, hearts, and bodies of women who were barely welcome back in their own villages, let alone in their own minds. I knew I had to be part of what they were doing.

I stood in line to meet him after the event wrapped up. He seemed convinced that he was much busier and more important than I was, and he made no effort to meet me. But I kept waiting. Finally I was the only person left, and I said these magic words: "I'm an attorney from the States.

My husband and I are here for ten months. And I'd be *really interested in volunteering.*"

His attention was suddenly laser-beam focused on me. "Can you start on Thursday?"

I started out as a volunteer and after three months was offered the position of counter-trafficking legal specialist. Pete and I had planned to be in Ukraine for only ten months but ended up staying for close to two and a half years so I could throw in my lot with these women and this work. Two and a half years of trainings with the former KGB, with non-profit NGOs devoted to empowering women, with churches looking to help returning victims of trafficking. Two and a half years of stories that cracked open my world to a crack that ran right through our world—this fissure in our natural faith in humanity. This ache because of a brokenness so perverse it makes you gag. This terrible, necessary work that taught me a new language, a new vocabulary, and a deeply satisfying sense of calling.

Near the end of my time in Ukraine, I sat with a woman at a table on the third floor of a UN building on Mykhailivska Street as she told around forty prominent leaders what it was like to be trafficked, sold. She was just a few years younger than I was, with blonde hair and perfect peach skin. She sat in a room full of men wearing the suits and the starched respectability of the various organizations they represented and talked naked truth. I sat next to her. I knew her story. It had the same ebb and flow of a hundred others I'd been hearing for two years and wouldn't ever be able to get out of my head.

I felt the familiar nausea. There are some things you can't force down your throat. Some acts the mind rejects. She kept talking in a quiet voice. I sometimes let my arm touch hers so she would know I was there, that I had her back. But she'd already lived braver than I could pretend to imagine. This was the woman and hers was the same story I'd spent two years learning from, writing grants for, advocating on behalf of, being introduced to over and over again. This was the work and the calling I believed I'd been built for. I was good at it.

• • •

Six years later, as I sat in an auditorium back in the States listening to a woman describe the counter-trafficking work of her mentor's organization, my heart burned and ached like my swollen jaw. But not for the reasons I was used to. I found myself incredulously discovering that all the passion and call and conviction that echoed around the room was still raging inside me, but instead of feeling it on behalf of women a world away, I now felt it on behalf of the small group of moms a table away who likely felt just as tired and confused at the juggle between kids and callings as I did.

I tapped my finger on one leg of my dark-blue pantsuit—the one I'd worn to court in Chicago, the one I'd worn with former KGB officers on law enforcement duty travel trips as they pursued facts for a prosecution or presented their experiences at a counter-trafficking seminar. I twisted and knotted my nervous fingers as my head kept up a running commentary with the God who had made me. I asked Him in the midst of so many people doing important, ground-breaking work to bring justice to the poor and hope to the afflicted if this new direction made sense. I showed Him this slow bubbling up from my insides, this belief that more needed to be done to speak into the lives of women—young mothers and wives who feel that what they do isn't important. Women who don't know how to balance their work, their mission, and their identities with the desire to have children. And who are told by many others that it isn't possible. Women who live in a quietly desperate suburban claustrophobia.

It was like finding buried treasure—discovering this unexpected part of me that wanted to champion moms, to encourage women through the mundane, hamster-wheel moments of their days. My heart was racing as the speaker wound down and I got to my feet with everyone else to applaud, to meet others around my table, to head up to my hotel room and bed. But before I made my way back, I caught a moment with the young woman who had introduced the keynote that night. After we exchanged backgrounds and friends in common, she surprised me by asking how old I was.

I laughed and told her the truth: "Thirty-five."

And then she wanted to know how many kids I had. When I told her two, she leaned in closer and asked, "How do you make it work?" She wanted to talk to me about kids. Not about trafficking or human rights or global justice, but about motherhood. And in a sea of suits discussing ways to change the world, two women stood with heads bent low over a conversation about if it's possible to fit babies into our lives as we know them, let alone into cross-cultural callings. If it is possible to have children and still live out your heart's desire to travel or to teach or to advocate or to make art, write, run, garden, or lead. If long-distance service in faraway places or living the life you love on the same block you grew up on is compatible with children.

"Yes," I told her over and over. Yes, children are adaptable, and a career and a calling to change lives across oceans or next-door fences does not disqualify you from motherhood. No, God doesn't ask us to trade who we are for the label of "Mom." Rather, He builds all the courage and calling of a lifetime into a story line big enough and rich enough to encompass kids, passion, work, creativity, and dreams that don't end in the labor and delivery ward.

And as I talked to her, it happened easily and naturally—this transition from advocating for one group of women (the ones I will always, passionately want to see liberated from trafficking) to advocating for another, no-less-important group (the tired moms, the wondering-if-they-can-be-moms women, the lost moms, the how-will-I-make-it-through-another-day mothers).

We parted ways, and I went upstairs in a daze, wondering if anyone could read the radical re-visioning of my life written across my face.

I remember staring at myself in the bathroom mirror. The bruises that had been green around the edges were darkening into purple blotches on my face. This face that had borne witness to precious lives of women lost to the lie of promised jobs in other countries, caught in the cross fire of poverty and people who traffic in human beings. This face that had been blank for years at the thought of children. This face that had been stunned at the arrival of a firstborn and then a second; this face that had crumbled and cried at the beauty of being reborn as a mother; this face that wanted nothing more now than to look deep into the eyes of tired women everywhere and tell them, "You are much braver than you think."

It was like finding a peephole into the heart of God—this discovering that He is never done writing our stories. That there will always be new plot twists up ahead. And at that moment, I sensed that He was looking right back at me without surprise—with only delight at this new turn.

I'd spent so long wanting to prove myself apart from the cliché of being someone's mother. I was stunned to find myself ready to champion mothers—arms wide open to the commissioning to speak life and encouragement and love into their lives. It may not be work on the level of the national news, but discovering that it mattered to the God who made me made it crucial. So I burrowed into that truth and crawled through it right into the place where God's call and my calling intersected.

I had to write it down. I opened my laptop in that hotel room at 2 a.m. and e-mailed my friend Holley. Nine months earlier I'd discovered the world of blogging—of sharing and connecting through our everyday stories. Holley was an online champion for the dreams of women, and I knew I could trust her with this shift in my story, so I wrote what was happening to me.

> I'm learning that this is why I blog. I write my heart out to this beautiful community that needs to be encouraged as I wish someone had done for me—to let each woman know that her only purpose isn't simply to have children, that God loves her for who she is and not just for what she can produce. But that if God leads her into a season of motherhood, then indeed that can be a glory in her life's work. That it's so much more than just a prerequisite. It's a partnership in a new identity that interprets her past and challenges her future. That young mothers and struggling women have great needs too. And that it is my delight to be used by God to be part of the plan for meeting them.

I hit send and brushed my teeth and got into bed with the peace of a woman who knows there will be no kids waking her up for milk in the middle of the night.

The next morning, my bruised jaw looked worse, and I kept having to explain to people that the fall was from chasing a five-year-old, not from a skiing accident, which would have been cooler and much less humiliating to cop to.

I boarded a plane that evening back to my real life and to a reunion spent spread eagled beneath a pile of flailing boy limbs as they leaped on top of me and loved me to the ground. And it felt like coming home in every sense of the word.

• • •

In the weeks following my return, it struck me with more force than ever before that I wasn't working in a human rights job anymore or regularly traveling overseas or thinking or speaking in any of my other languages. After our two and a half years in Ukraine, I'd transitioned to advocating for housing justice for orphans and vulnerable children in South Africa, and then when we first moved back to the States, I still did consulting in this kind of work. But since our move to DC, I'd left that work behind. I was living in a small rental house in a middle-class neighborhood with a commute through crazy-making traffic for two hours to and from an uninspired job each day, with painful preschool and day care drop-offs and pickups on either end.

Like many other women, I got up while it was still dark to provide for my family, and on many days, it was harder than anything else I'd done. Micah would climb into the bed in the predawn hours, and we would cocoon under the covers together until it was time to stop hitting snooze. Then he would pad up the hallway after me, squint against the bright bathroom lights, and come in to sit on the toilet seat lid as I showered and applied makeup. He stayed close to me, savoring the wee hours we shared together.

And in the evenings, when the kids had been wrestled and fed and bathed and lathered and rinsed, and each had had a chance to whisper the secrets of his days into my ear, I'd crawl under the yellow duvet cover we'd had for years and carve out time to listen to and embrace the stories of other moms shared across blogs and miles—connected by a passion to find more than exhaustion at the end of our days.

Those days taught me to pray. Those days taught me that it's okay to hurt in the tension. That it's normal to ask all the "Why?" and "What's next?" questions. And that sometimes we're called to keep walking forward anyway—without answers, with only the blind assurance that we are beloved.

For a year after I discovered this unexpected passion to encourage other mothers with all the words I wished someone had said to me when I was my most lost as a new mom, I felt like a pitcher—full to the brim, but with nowhere and no one to pour into. I would wake up and go to work and come home and make supper and love my kids and my man and go to bed still feeling like my pitcher hadn't quite found the emptying it needed. It was a long, frustrating wait. But a few nights a week, I poured out words into the vastness of the Internet about my everyday struggles to find my balance as a mom, and when I went to bed, I discovered that I'd given away a little something.

After a while, the words turned into a steady stream, and some of them filled glasses at other tables. I was still working at a job that didn't seem to fit me, but at night I was pouring the most satisfying encouragement into other women and discovering the wonder of being filled up by their words as well. The website (in)courage was one of those places. Holley and her cofounder, Stephanie, invited me to write with them—to join them and twenty-eight other women in the calling to encourage the hearts of women. We all saw (in)courage as a bit like a beach house—a place where women could feel welcome without pretense, valued just the way they are. A place where we could put our sandy, dirty feet up on the coffee table and tell our real, hard stories. A place where people would listen. A place where women were brave enough to be vulnerable.

Pouring into (in)courage emptied me and left me feeling satisfied. And when I wrote about my everyday, ordinary mess, I felt connected to the women I wanted to encourage. The women I wanted to wrap arms around and laugh with and say, "You're doing far more than just okay, sister."

It turned out that this thing—this something else that I had been waiting for—had been unfolding in my life all along. Right there in the commuter lane, in between making school snack packs and tucking kids into bed, I'd been finding my voice. God was making a way for me through the frustration and into the nooks and crannies of other people's stories. All the while making sense of my own—every step, every twist, every turn along the way.

GOD BUILDS ALL THE COURAGE AND CALLING
OF A LIFETIME INTO A STORY LINE
BIG ENOUGH AND RICH ENOUGH
to encompass kids, passion,
work, creativity, and dreams
that don't end in the labor
and delivery ward.

and then after eighteen years, I rediscovered my mom

PEOPLE OFTEN ASK how many kids you plan to have. We never had a plan. Although we knew that we weren't done at two. But never once did I suspect it might be a daughter. I was the girl with two brothers and a dad, the girl whose mom had died. I was the girl who was comfortable around guys. I was the mom who had two sons, and even the kids we sponsored through Compassion International were boys. So when I got a sneaking suspicion that it was time to take a pregnancy test, the only pink I was expecting were the two lines that showed up in the test window.

We hadn't been trying for a baby. But we hadn't been not trying either. And for two weeks I'd suspected what the test would confirm. So new, so delicate, so unexpected, I barely even whispered it to myself. And on an otherwise ordinary Wednesday, on the morning of my thirty-sixth birthday, the day I mourned eighteen years and half a lifetime lived without my mother, I finally took the test. I watched it turn positive on the blue sink of an old bathroom and heard Jesus whisper, "Life!" Always He remakes. Always He knits together what is separated, fractured, to create wholeness.

And isn't this just like Him? To be going about His beautiful business while we go about ours, oblivious. Quietly, in the secret places, He works and plans and prepares a future for us that is spun from our DNA and His Spirit. His eyes never sleep and His hands are never idle, and He admires His handiwork and grins to Himself in the wee hours while we sleep. And He whispers His eternal refrain: "It is good. It is good. It is very good."

And I am His creature who He invited to cocreate life with Him, and I will never forget how we laughed together—I at the unexpectedness of it all, and He, it seemed, at my surprise. And I wrapped my arms around myself and knew that the mother who wasn't there to wrap hers was wrapping them tight, tight nonetheless. Because she now knows His goodness firsthand and sings with the seraphim, "Holy, holy, holy." And in my upside-down house, I stood on holy ground right there between the sink and the toilet seat of a seafoam-blue bathroom from the seventies that had seen better days.

I waited for a moment to tell Peter. Not for a perfect moment—just a quiet moment would do. But first there was family-night dinner with his students, and then on the way home the boys were a raucous, exhausted haze. The car was rattling, and I told Pete it had been making me nervous all day. He pulled over to the slow lane, and we shuddered and finally pulled off the five-lane highway into our neighborhood. And right then, just two streets from home, we watched as our left front tire bounced off the car and across the road in front of us. The white, hand-me-down Grand Marquis from my father-in-law grated to a screeching halt as its left shoulder buried into the blacktop, and we saw a driver in front of us pull over and chase down our runaway tire. A police car was right behind us, and he put on his lights so no one would hit us from behind.

And it was afterward—after a neighbor had come to pick up the boys and me in his truck, after Pete had dealt with the tow truck and the body shop and the insurance reports, after the kids were in bed and he had sat down on the couch across from me, rattling off our options, running his hands through his hair, that I found a moment to tell him. Right into the chaos and the noise of a life that had spanned nearly two decades, I told him without any romantic flourishes.

"Well, I think we're going to need a bigger car anyway. For all the car seats."

He was running his hands through that thick head of hair. "Maybe. But maybe we just sit tight till we're ready for another baby and then we get the minivan."

"I think we need the minivan now," I told him.

"But we're okay for now, I think." He hadn't heard me. "I

just talked to my dad, and there are a lot of small options that will do just fine till we're sure we need something bigger."

"I think we need something bigger today," I said.

He slowly looked up from the floor.

"Wait, what?" His fingers came to a standstill in his hair.

"I think we need the big car, like, now," I said. And the grin I'd been holding in all day finally surfaced.

Peter started to laugh. Peter with his dark hair all sprinkled with salt and pepper started to laugh the same chuckle I'd loved since I was twenty-one.

"Are you telling me what I think you're telling me?"

"Yup. Happy birthday to me, and we need a minivan."

And then we were both laughing—best friends who had seen pretty much everything together. And this was one more milestone I'll always remember through his eyes. My husband, my Michigan boy, the father of this surprising baby, who was nodding and saying over and over, "Of course. Of course, because, just of course."

• • •

A week later I went to Guatemala with Compassion International, and the secret went with me. With the sun rising above the glinting jet planes, I sat at my departure gate and did what I always do before I fly—I called my dad in South Africa.

I caught him on his knees in his study. The fine line between his laughter and his tears was blurred as always as he prayed for my journey, and I stored up his words in my heart. His voice echoed all around me and cupped me safe in the embrace of the Father who bridged the ocean between us.

And I didn't care what the other travelers thought as slow tears made their way down my face at the long-distance blessing. He prayed for new DNA to be imprinted with this first mission trip. He prayed for cells to be intertwined with service. He prayed courage for us both.

I boarded.

We boarded.

And I knew there was a heart of darkness that would eat the world if it could. I knew about loss and separation and homesickness. I knew there was poverty smeared across the faces of children and stamped into the hearts of the wealthy that only grace can erase. I knew we live in a broken world that groans as it waits to be rescued.

But I believed rescue would come. I believed it was already coming. And sometimes it is heralded by the dividing of two cells. There is life and light in the darkness. And the darkness has not understood it. And the darkness cannot put it out.

So I flew on the wings of the morning, God's grace, and my father's prayers to introduce the third of my children to that most sacred of opportunities—seeing the world through someone else's eyes.

●　●　●

The third time around was the best of the three because I could see what was coming from a long way off. I could anticipate. On a practical level, I had all the clothes and the toys. And I'd adapted to sleep deprivation. But people kept asking me if we were hoping for a girl. And it irritated me because I wanted a boy. I wanted three boys, my own small tribe. A band of brothers. I loved everything about that idea. I hushed the notion of a girl. I raised an eyebrow at inquisitive checkout ladies who asked if this third time around was our last-ditch effort for a girl, told them bluntly, "No, actually, I'm rooting for another boy."

And I was. I wouldn't know where to start with a girl. The thought terrified me.

But God. God knits babies together in the secret dark. And we can plan all we like, but we have no actual control over the outcomes. We bear witness to the miracle, and we women—we also bear it in our bodies. But we certainly don't dictate it. Small wonder that to get a glimpse into their secret world, we need to go into darkened rooms lit only by a flickering screen to read what we can of who they are becoming.

But God already knows. He already delights. He has already been singing over them in the dark, secret hours of spinning life out of strands of DNA—an artist at work, creating and shaping another Adam-child in His image. And the sonogram is desperate to catch up. The black-and-white shifting dimensions on the screen only hint at His handiwork. At the brilliance and the raw beauty beating with the brand-new chambers of a heart there on the dim screen.

It is the shape the Father sculpted in the beginning and the shape the Christ-Son took. It is the ancient, familiar form that is still somehow new every time we see it fitted over a new soul. Upward and forward and deeper into the heart of God with each new life He entrusts us with. Parts of us crack wide open, and we are vulnerable to a vast army of fears, for to parent is to ache over the unknown. And this third time I felt the ache like a low register in the small of my back. In the past five years I'd had too many friends who lost their children in ways the brain can barely process. Children crushed under pickup trucks, children lost in the womb, children who couldn't live outside the shelter of their mother's bodies.

I watched them try to jigsaw-puzzle their lives back together. I no longer took anything for granted. All is grace. All is undeserved gift. I saw the miracle now with both eyes wide, wide open.

And one afternoon in Fairfax, Virginia, a sonogram tech pointed at a black-and-white picture and told me that our miracle was a daughter.

A girl. I was going to have a girl.

• • •

It took me nine months to wrap my head around it. I didn't own anything pink. And I was scared. I didn't have the vocabulary for girls. I didn't understand the wardrobe. I was lost before it even began and frustrated that God would get things so wrong to send this broken-down daughter of His a daughter to mother. I was sure I wouldn't be able to do right by her.

But pregnancy is never in a rush. It gives us slow months to sort through all the changes. And this time around, more of them would have to unfold in my head than in my womb. Which was saying something. Because I read Pete page after page of unattractive pregnancy symptoms I'd skipped the first two times around that came a-calling with a vengeance for my third.

Friends kept telling me it would be okay. That I'd love her. Of course I'd love her. But my heart was wrung out with doubt, and it was hard to swallow past my sense of inadequacy.

But then her name found me—like a blessing, like a promise, like a secret whispered between friends.

I was thirty-seven weeks pregnant and putting together salad for lunch, sprinkling dressing, cutting soft French bread between the red toaster and the red bread box in my messy kitchen when I heard it. The word He'd spoken on the eighteenth anniversary of my mother's death, before I'd known there was a *daughter* growing inside of me. Before I recognized her, He already knew. And so He spoke life on the day I mourned half a lifetime without my mother. It was on that same day that Jesus spoke life over me and into me.

Now, months later, I was sure of her name. Zoe. The Greek word for "life"—so much unexpected life that He'd given us. I felt her kicking inside me. And I was a living altar of remembrance to what He had done. God was with me, in me, and I was in Him. Life and grace. Even when I was not aware of it. Maybe especially then.

I set down the knife and its glob of butter on the fading laminate counter, and I could hear the chorus playing of how much Jesus loved me. Playing loud and here and just for me in between the sink and the faux bricks that kept falling off the rental house's wall. *How am I worthy of this love?* The girl who grew up believing she was nothing apart from her ability to reproduce, so wounded by that gospel that she swore off marriage and children, now standing here beloved and pregnant and in a pool of grace as warm as the sunshine pouring through the window.

How did He do it?

How did He take the most broken bits of my childhood and all their jagged edges and fit them together in this tremendous testimony to His patient love? Somehow He soldered them into a stained-glass whole and made my story beautiful. The motherless daughter was now cocreating a girl-child with the God who never demanded it from her, who only offered it as a free gift.

I am His art. And with Him, we make art together. Living art. Life. And only because of His grace. Zoe Grace. Life and Grace. This is my testimony.

• • •

I was scheduled for a C-section. After the run both boys had given me, my doctors agreed that trying normal childbirth again was not worth the risk of a fourth-degree episiotomy. I wholeheartedly agreed. So her date was circled on the calendar, and life continued in its everyday rhythm around us. March brought spring and Amiee, an old friend I'd known since law school. She'd moved back to DC and was on call for the day I was scheduled to deliver. But Zoe was not mine to plan, even in this detail, and two days before her due date, I went into labor.

It was a Saturday morning. The boys had both snuck into bed with us. We'd been potty training Micah for months, and he had all but mastered it except for the occasional nighttime accident. I allowed him into the bed under threat of what would happen to him if he wet our mattress. Again.

He was cavalier. Climbed in with his *Cars* pajamas and snuggled between Peter and me. Jackson was on his other side. Spring was easing through the blinds, and we could hear the birds. And then I felt it—the telltale wetness seeping into the mattress. I turned on Micah, and he was all big eyes and denials until I realized that the water was coming from me.

I jumped out of the bed, if *jump* is the right word for a woman in her thirty-ninth week of pregnancy, and water poured down my legs. The boys were dying. Micah was pointing, all fingers and accusation. "It's Mom! Mom wet the bed!"

And I was laughing so hard I couldn't find the breath to respond. Pete was suddenly sitting straight upright, and he yelled, "No, it's Zoe. The baby's coming, guys. The baby's coming."

The boys clambered out from under the covers and started fist-pumping and leaping on the bed, yelling in unison with their dad, "The baby's coming, the baby's coming," as I clutched a towel between my legs and felt the familiar bubble of awe burst inside my chest.

The on-call doctor said we'd better come in and check things out, so I called Amiee next. At 8 a.m. on a Saturday morning. I may always owe her for that. But she came right over, and I was wearing a pink shirt and black sweatpants, and she took a photo of Peter and me outside the house, next to the tall tree and at least one or two discarded plastic rakes and shovels. I felt like I'd swallowed spring. We left Amiee with directions to the nearest park, snack packs to feed the guys, instructions about nap times, and promises to text as soon as the baby arrived.

We got hold of Pete's parents and texted friends, but I couldn't get through to my dad. By the time we arrived at the hospital, I was grateful for all the pre-registration rigmarole we'd been through, because it meant I didn't need to wait. I just walked my early stages of labor directly to the elevator and the maternity ward.

It's such holy territory—this tender care for women who arrive weighed down by the wonder and the ache of new children. All these nurses and doctors ready to catch the future. They put me in a bed, hooked me up to a monitor, called for the anesthesiologist to come and talk to me about the C-section and how it would go down. In between talking to him, I was trying to get through to my dad, who was in a remote part of South Africa with bad reception. The nurses watching my hardening contractions told me it was nearly time to go. And Pete kept pressing redial for me, because I couldn't have a baby without talking to the man who had delivered me, only daughter of my mother.

Then his voice was coming down the line, clear as if he were standing beside the bed, holding my hand.

"Lisa-Jo? My darling! My baby. Go with Jesus. You're going to meet your baby girl. You can do it. Oh, I remember on a morning like this, thirty-seven years ago in Zululand, how I met you, my daughter. We love you. We love you. It's time to hurl you down the track. We're cheering for you."

And of course he prayed. A blessing from the heart of the karoo dirt, and I received it with both hands, crying and not caring how many nurses came in and adjusted the IV in my arm or rolled up the sides of the bed to move me to the delivery room or overheard my father praying for the doctor who would cut, the doctor who would catch, the granddaughter who would arrive. He prayed and my faith got brave, and when I hung up, the team was in a rush to roll me down the corridor ahead of the contractions that were gaining momentum. It went down so fast. Without a hard labor to fight through first, it was so fast.

I was lying with arms spread wide on the delivery table, a nurse leaning over me and looking me in the eyes, watching every breath and making sure I was talking, connecting, ready. I was. As they prepped me, the on-call doctor said he'd heard I was from South Africa, that I'd talked to my dad. In a sterile delivery room in northern Virginia, he asked me about the country that holds my heart. He asked me about the land that smells like dust and bleeds purple every October with the jacaranda trees. In the season of American cherry blossoms, I told him about my home under the eaves of the purple trees. And that my father had prayed for him. Not that he doubted his ability, but rather that he'd prayed a blessing on all of us. And the doc looked at me over his mask, smiled around the room, and said, "Well, I guess it's going to be a good delivery when you've been prayed for all the way from South Africa." And he cut me open.

Pete was at my head, his face so close to mine I could almost feel him breathing. I asked them to tell me when they could see her. So the doc, he kept up a running narrative.

"I can see the uterus."

"I'm at the outer layer."

"I'm through now."

"You'll feel some tugging here. A hard pull."

"Okay, you're about to meet your daughter. Here she comes. Here she comes now."

And the next voice I heard was Zoe's. Mewling like a loud, angry kitten, she was lifted high up in the air above me, then carried across the room. I sent Pete with her because it was so far to have her travel without me. They weighed and suctioned and warmed and wrapped her and then brought the gift back to me. She looked like a small papoose, wrapped up so tight. They laid her cheek to cheek with me, and after being lost for so long, I felt like I was opening my arms to a daughter and finding in my hands a compass.

Zoe. From her first breath, I was drawn back into the

rhythm of life. Life not for carpooling or playdates or grocery shopping. Life not for who forgot to put the wash into the dryer or vacuum the living room. Life not for "Take your muddy shoes off *before* you walk into the house!"

But life for life.

For life first.

For life alone.

Beat by beat. Breath by breath.

The whole symphony of lungs heaving and blood drumming in her veins and breaths drawn deep and gasped back out in those first, tiny sounds. Life for fists clenched hard and fingers unfurled slow. Life traveling down a million nerve endings with messages to open, to breathe, to beat, to warm, to clot, to protect, to live. To *live*. Life raw and pounding in my ears and down my cheeks as she wakened to the world a blink away from me.

> I have come that they may have life, and have it to
> the full.
>
> JOHN 10:10

I cradled it in my arms—all this new life. Dark, black, unfocused eyes looked back at me. The Creator's Spirit lingered on her skin, in her hair. There was a reverence in the air; she was still so fresh from the making, from the passing of His hands to mine. And me—I was so aware of my rough, scuffed self with skin stained from years of living on this silent planet that only stubbornly, in fits and starts, acknowledges its Maker.

I held her and listened to her breathe. I listened to her drink life from my body to hers. She gulped it in rhythmic swallows. This was the gift. That even though I was broken and my soul stained, the Creator still invited me to cocreate and sustain life with Him. I am His daughter. She is mine. We are both grafted into His heartbeat. And I never wanted it to be over.

Not the nursing or the changing or the rocking. Not the dark wee hours when I fumbled for glasses and sighed through her soft whimpers as I had to get up again and again and again. Because then there she was, curled up into the crook of my arm with a chubby leg hanging just so over my hand. I ran my fingers over her toes. They curled around and into my palm.

The love beat was so loud in those quiet moments in a hospital room and then in her own small room at our house that I was certain she must hear it too. The blood pumping a drumbeat dance of the great mother love that sings down through the ages and ululates a wild love cry over this tiny daughter of mine. The dark cocooned us both and the rocking chair whispered and she drank and I cupped her head. I bowed low over the silver sheen from that tiny halo of hair. And inside something worshiped—something broke wide open, and I was certain my chest could not contain this emotion. This wonder at being a fingerprint in God's palm as He created and cast a life into being.

She knew. She watched me from under half-closed lashes

in between gulps and breaths, and my eyes told her, *Yes, yes I was part of your making.* I was her beginning, and in every way that this pockmarked history of being a daughter adrift from a mother had scarred me, she was my new beginning too.

Blood beat. Daughter drank. Spirit exhaled. I held that hand and found that she held me. All that the deceiver sought to rob me of, all my daughterhood lost for years, was soothed and restored by those five chubby fingers. Then slowly, with the creaking limbs of one who knows the value of silence at midnight, I unwound her from myself and eased her back into her crib. And there it was—the soft sigh of a baby full and content. My benediction.

• • •

But I carried a suitcase stuffed full of the heavy memories I wished my own mom had done differently. And one Sunday morning when my daughter was less than six months old, the lock on that suitcase broke right open and exploded onto the bed in a riot of insecurity among the four different outfits I made her try on before church.

I'd worried for a long time that I would not be a good mother to a daughter. My heart was pounding and I could feel it—the impending sense of letting her down. How many nights had I whispered into the deep blue of her eyes how beautiful I thought she was? I said it now, at the beginning of things, so her life would be colored with those words. So there would be no doubt in her mind that her mother thought her beautiful. I held tight to those words like a seal I could put over her heart, before any boy could get there. Before any other words could find their way past the door, I wanted *beautiful* to be sealed up tight in the house of her heart.

I know firsthand the ways to splinter a daughter's heart with the fumbling of that one word.

So I panicked because on that day of all days, old splinter scars throbbed as I tried to choose clothes for her, my beautiful daughter. She needed the right clothes because that day I had to put on Hannah's shoes and walk into the house of God and give Zoe back to Him. That day we would dedicate her in church in front of God and His people, and I was terrified that I would get it wrong.

I was terrified that there, at the beginning of the moments in her life that mattered, I would be at a loss to dress her on the outside with the beauty that lived on the inside—that I would fail this test of mothering a daughter. I wasn't the girl with the fashion sense. I was the girl with the brothers and the dead mother, and I didn't know how to do right by her when it came to clothes.

Why should it matter? I heard myself asking as I tossed aside the short-sleeved, pink gingham dress with the tiny cross-stitched flowers.

Why did I care so much that the white dress with the scalloped edges was too wide around her arms and the Onesie underneath was the wrong color?

Who cares? Who cares? It's just clothing!

But it's not. It's years of wondering how the popular girls

blow-dried their hair so effortlessly and managed to wear jeans that showed off all the right curves, while I drowned in sizes always too big, too awkward, too ordinary on my too-thin and bony frame.

Whether or not people thought I was beautiful, I rarely *felt* beautiful.

I was desperate to give her a better head start in the race against the world's opinion of women.

Zoe, your mother will be the one to cement the word beauty into the foundation of who you are so that, come the teenage years, come acne and growth spurts, cliques and boys, you will not doubt that your beauty is deeper than all of that.

My daughter, how has God trusted me with this great weight of responsibility? I am afraid I will fail Him and you on a Sunday morning because I cannot seem to pick the right thing for you to wear.

• • •

We dedicated her.

We dedicated her back to Jesus.

And I stood in a row of people I loved who have known me since before I knew her father. And even though I had chosen right, and the pale-pink skirt that draped all the way down to her pink Mary Janes was perfect, we sang the words that put everything we wore and everything that we were into the proper perspective:

What a wonderful Maker . . .
You made the world and saw that it was good.

He made her. He made her, and that makes her so good. No matter what her mother does or doesn't do.

I stood with my arms so full of the weight of His goodness that they ached, and there was an imprint forming on my inner arm.

I held a small world in my arms, and I celebrated the God who made her and called her good. And in that moment, I was at peace with being her mother and her being my daughter, and I whispered to my mom, "Look, I have a girl. *Look*." And the eighteen years since she died washed away in the worship.

I had a daughter.

I had a daughter.

I would mother a girl-child, and it would be a wonder.

And right then, the words of the God who had made all three of us came up on the screen, and the world made sense as the Father God whispered to us, His daughters:

Why do you worry about clothes? See how the flowers of the field grow. They do not labor or spin. Yet I tell you that not even Solomon in all his splendor was dressed like one of these. If that is how God clothes the grass of the field, which is here today and tomorrow is thrown into the fire, will he not much more clothe you?

MATTHEW 6:28-30

And I heard it—the Zulu word that echoed from across the ocean and home.

Sibahle.

The word that means "we are beautiful."

• • •

Zoe has become my teacher. She teaches me about how mothers love their daughters. My tiny, blonde-haired tutor, she toddles toward me with chubby hands cupped full of LEGOs, her brothers' toy soldiers, and life. A baby doll is tucked under her arm, her gap-toothed grin declaring, "I am impossible to forget." The living that busts out of every ounce of that kid fills up corners of our family we didn't know were empty. The angle of my world has shifted, and without taking my eyes off Zoe, I find myself staring backwards through time and watching my mother watch me.

I see the first year stitched together with rocking chair nights. I see a heart that didn't know it was daughter empty; a soft, yellow knitted blanket; a giraffe lovey tucked behind blonde curls each night.

I see the crawling and the climbing on furniture and up and down three cement steps and through the dirt.

I see the gummy grins and Oupa playing with his first granddaughter.

I see the outline of a school uniform and brown shoes with a too-big backpack waving good-bye on the way to grade one.

I see a seven-year-old with mousy brown hair, much taller

than her petite ballet companions, twirling the moves she makes up in her imagination.

I see a twelve-year-old worried about fitting into her skin and riding her bike to a new school. I see her playing netball and growing out her bangs and writing poems in the back of her math book.

I see her at sixteen. She is beautiful. All girl and all woman and all caught in the in-between.

I see her at eighteen as she spins in a royal-blue dress, leaving her mother far behind.

And then I see Zoe through the outlines of me, and I know that at eighteen she will have hardly drawn the breath of living memory. I will have lived a hundred lifetimes of love for her by then. Eighteen is too short to know a mother. Eighteen is a deep well of knowing a daughter.

I am thirty-eight and Zoe is two, and already I have more of her saved up than could be recorded in any library. So I know now what I didn't know then: we weren't strangers, my mother and I. The memory lapses are one sided: *You always knew me, didn't you, Mom?* Like I know the dimple in Zoe's right cheek. And how she breathes out loudly through her nose when she's processing a strong emotion. Or how she likes to stroke my arm as she falls asleep tucked into my chest.

Mothering Zoe, I have unwittingly stepped into the shoes of Jo and find there memories with deep, rich roots. My daughter—she is growing me up into a mom and into a daughter who remembers she was beloved all eighteen years, starting at the first one.

ALWAYS GOD REMAKES.
Always He knits together
what is separated, fractured,
to create wholeness.

CHAPTER 13

jesus loves me this I know, for my children taught me so

My BODY BEARS testimony to the children it has borne. In the curve of my waist and the set of my hips there is a love song that lisps the words of that old children's hymn: "Jesus loves me this I know." I stand naked, as God and Peter see me, before the full-length mirror we bought after I delivered Zoe, and I run my hands over the aches and dips and round curves of life that this body spells. It reflects memories and growth, and it is my living Ebenezer—the reminder that great love is always born from great sacrifice.

Like a secret whispered between old friends, there is the scar that stitched Zoe into the world, a thin, white finger of numbness running low across my abdomen. I enfold it with my hands, and it's a prayer, these two palms pressed down on the place where she entered the world, begging the God who gave her to me to keep her safe, to carry her now when I cannot. Isn't all motherhood this one great prayer that rises in a thousand different languages: "Let them be loved and let them be safe"?

My fingers trail up to my belly button, and it makes me smile how it winks at me from a tummy much fuller than it was when we started this journey eight years ago. Jackson filled that waist with the rich, nourishing acceptance that a skinny eighteen-year-old once lacked. He knit three countries together for us. We fell in love with the idea of him in Ukraine and raced daylight and schedules to sneak through a window of opportunity like two teenagers on a reckless summer night, high on fireflies and expectation.

Sex as an act of creation, of art, of life, filled our thoughts and bed and intertwined the parts of us we didn't realize we'd still been living separate. This righteous act of love that reminds human creatures that there is a miracle wrapped in the gift of pleasure. A miracle that points to a good Gift Giver outside ourselves, outside our control, outside our timelines, outside our attempts at manipulation or desperate demands. Galaxies must align and collide in the secret dark, and all we can do is humble ourselves to be available to something much bigger than our comprehension. This sigh of letting go sounds like the echo of a God who created first and creates last and lingers over us with the tender, terrifying words, "Let there be . . ."

We had packed our hopes and our passion with us when we left Ukraine and planned to be in the States for Christmas before we settled back in South Africa. And it was on Christmas Eve morning in Moline, Illinois, that I woke up at five and stepped gingerly over creaking floorboards and into the bathroom between the four upstairs bedrooms and took the test that sent me to my knees on the white bathroom mat. Clutching my belly, I put my forehead on the floor, bowed low at the wonder and the awe of what was happening inside of me that was so outside my control. I was nauseous at the thought. You can think you want something and then be terrified when it shows up in your bloodstream.

Jackson Jo. My firstborn, my undoing, my remaking, my gift. I have gained pounds and gray hair since I gained you.

The mirror is smudged with his prints and a hundred memories of him posing and flexing and laughing at his reflection. I saw him first as a small red Onesie I ran out to buy at Target after I took that pregnancy test. It had green piping and the words "My First Christmas" written across the chest. It was the gift and the news we gave his grandparents and great-grandparents and carried with us across Illinois and into Michigan and Wisconsin, surprising aunts and uncles each time it was unwrapped for Christmas. Christ with us as we shared the news of miracle and wonder. Jackson knit me into the fiber and DNA and story of the Baker family, and his face reflects his father. How much I love him for that, my son, my child transplanted from snowy shores and born under the jacarandas and into the bosom of South Africa. He laid me low. He built a bridge between my broken past and my new beginning.

The woman who looks back at me from the mirror is someone I never expected to meet. There she is, with her tired eyes and wrinkle lines and the soft brown spots of aging on her hands. Her hair hasn't been its own color since she turned nineteen. She prefers a shade of auburn colored into the mix. She is comfortable in her skin. I like her. I like the life she has lived. The stories she has written. The names she carries like so much dirt under her fingernails from digging into the roots of a family. She calls back easily to the warbled, two-syllable song of "Mama!" that rises from the backyard, where the boys are upending the wheelbarrow, dumping sand out of the sandbox, digging more holes where there once was grass. She can see them from the window that slides open beside the mirror, the one that Jackson broke with a baseball just months back—a sacred milestone in mothering boys.

Where Micah and Jackson are, there Zoe goes also, wielding her own toy gun while carrying a baby doll tucked safely beneath the other arm. She puts her shoes on the wrong feet and won't quit calling Jackson "Guy" and repeating Micah's name over and over until he is fit to bust and she knows she has his full attention. Micah mutters beneath his breath because he knows I won't condone it: "I hate this baby!" Yet he is the first one to reach her side anytime she falls down, scrapes a knee, calls for help.

Micah Peter. I was cut and I bled to bring you into this world more than any other. You have taught me what brave looks like.

There are some scars in such private places that we don't even let our minds look too closely at them. This body bears witness to the naked truth that our children will hurt us. They will push and push as hard against us as the day we delivered them into the world. And my wrinkles, the creases in my forehead—they are from nights spent in a rocking chair or crouched next to the bottom bunk under the white Christmas lights strung from above, praying for a way to make sense of his world.

We see ourselves in our children better than in any mirror. And Micah is my warrior-son with all the passion of his Viking ancestors beating through his veins and drumming like a headache in my temples. The temper I inherited from my father lives in the five-year-old fast asleep in his superhero Underoos on the bottom bunk, and I lay hands on him and pray for us both. I didn't know I was selfish until I had kids. I didn't know I was angry and quick to keep a list of wrongs done to me, of slight slights, of everything I felt entitled to and was happy to demand.

Peter has fought many a long, losing battle with me, as pointless and exhausting as the rounds I have gone with Micah over whether he eats breakfast from the blue or the red bowl. But I believe God loves us too much to leave us flailing in our self-centered universes, so He delivers these tiny reflections of ourselves into our homes with earthquake effectiveness. The walls and the ground shift as we are forced to rearrange our sleep, our interests, our books, our date nights, our bathroom habits, our love of hot food, our blankets, our vacation plans, our entertainment choices, our interests, our bodies, our patience, and the grip on our sanity into unrecognizable new patterns.

Micah, who arrived two days after Christmas, was the most memorable and hard-won Christmas gift I've ever received. The nurses in that Michigan maternity ward watched over me with wide eyes as the snow fell outside, and they brought me ice packs made from hollowed-out newborn diapers. I was embarrassed at how hard my labor had been until Dr. Chavez arrived to visit me and my son—he with the swelling hematoma on the back of his head where the suction had worked to pull him free from my body. My doctor sat on the edge of the bed and told me how brave I'd been. And when friends from our home group arrived just moments later, he told them, too.

And I tended my bloodied, victorious body and my boy. His fight continued when he was readmitted for jaundice, and then four weeks later, when he was back in the hospital with a terrifying bout of RSV and inhibited breathing, reminding me over and over, *Oh God, how I need You. I can't gasp a single breath on my own apart from this body You breathed life into. May I never be free of the umbilical cord that anchors me, childlike, to Your side, because I am terrified to do this life alone.*

I see in Micah how God loves me, how He gave up heaven and Himself for me. How He spread His arms wide to ridicule and suffering, to gasps and agony and wanting it to be over and wanting to be released from this calling that cost

Him so much. This salvation, this redemption, this act of bearing children of the new covenant from His body through the mighty act of adoption and delivery on a cross.

I kneel beside my sleeping son, and I would do it all over again—the uncertainty, the battles to understand him, the temper and the challenge, the brokenness and the stubbornness, and the desperate ache that requires me to step into his world and pour myself out as a love offering, freely given with no expectation of payback. A gift. I lay myself down for my son who is learning to love because I first loved him. And his love has come back like an avalanche, a tornado. Ten thousand times anything I have been hurt, I have been healed because of this boy who has taught me what it looks like to see redemption in the reflection of great sacrifice.

Every night I tuck him in and I pray with him and his brother and bring the last glass of water and adjust the music and fix the blankets and find the missing lovey and answer "just one more" question until inevitably I say, "Mom is done, boys; I'm just done now. No one gets out again, understand?" And they nod and watch me with big eyes and come padding out of their room just minutes later nonetheless, with tentative faces and bare chests and whisper, "We just want to hug you again."

Some nights I sigh. Some nights I rant. Some nights I'm already in bed and too tired to do more than just open my arms. Those nights are the best, because the boys clamber between the covers and my limbs, and we pretzel one more time, outlined by the dying day like we did when they were so much smaller, and then they slip away back to bed, bending first to kiss me on the forehead. *Keep coming,* I want to tell them. *And I will keep opening my arms, and we will keep teaching each other what it looks like to give up the pieces of ourselves we thought we needed, in order to make room for someone else.*

Because when we least expect it or want it, God is always pouring more of His own life into our lives, and we need to open both arms wide if we want to even begin to try to hold it all.

Zoe Grace. You are the exclamation point, the bookend, the bracket, the bright rim of the sun rising over my mothering discovery. I give you my story, Zoe, and this legacy of womanhood beloved, womanhood celebrated, womanhood redeemed. Daughter of mine, daily grace.

Where I began lost, I end found in the small palm of her hand. Where I was broken and cracked open, I am healed and pieced together discovering my reflection as both mother and daughter in her eyes. Where I was hurt, I am whole watching her watch me and knowing we will write a new story of womanhood together. It will be good, and it will begin again and again and again each morning when I walk into her room and she throws her arms wide open to me and the day and her family and the fifteen stuffed animals in her bed and lisps, "I wuv you *so* much, Mama."

This face that watches me from the mirror knows what faith feels like beneath her feet—this substance of things unseen. I read it with my fingers, braille written in the lives of my children. How they teach me to pray, "For Yours is the Kingdom and the power and the glory forever." They teach me to pray. They teach me grace. They teach me again and again, with each new morning and each preschool appointment and each temper tantrum, and when we take off the training wheels, and as we see a hundred days unfold on Joplin Street behind the white walls of the rental house I never wanted. This life that is now so much more than my own. *Teach us to pray. Let Your Kingdom come; let Your will be done, on earth as it is in heaven.*

The tulips we planted our first fall in this house five years ago keep coming up each spring, though I've done nothing to help them, nothing to feed them, nothing to invite them. There they are anyway, nodding pink, red, yellow heads at the glory that arrives like so much daily bread—undeserved and beautiful each spring. And like His children so many centuries before, I wake up and I ask, "Father, what is it?" Because I can't believe all this manna He leaves for me to gather by the basketful.

Zoe wraps her arms around me as I wrap a bath towel around her, her giggles as fresh and enchanting as her curls. Micah cups crushed dandelions in his pocket to deliver to me along with all the mud in the neighborhood that has arrived with his sneakers. And Jackson dances and dances and dances like a mother I once knew who ran out under cover from a rainstorm and danced on a wild karoo farm garden until her children couldn't resist and ran out into the joy with her, heads tilted back and mouths open to the wonder. She may be buried in the big *veld vlakte* behind that garden now, but we have none of us forgotten how to dance.

"Again," says Zoe. "Again." And it's her anthem of delight. It's the refrain that comes back over and over as we spin in the living room, as we ride scooters around the block, as Pete wrestles her or kisses her or gives her pony rides on the bed. "Again," and indeed again the sun rises and my hips widen and I have carried babies three times in the long dance of motherhood and made peanut butter sandwiches and nursed colds and soothed fevers and walked miles of carpet and climbed into bed each night beside the boy from Michigan with the cowboy eyes who started it all.

Lying next to him, holding his hand, tucked into the curve of his thigh, I am home no matter what country I am in—this love that cracks the lock on zip codes and time zones. This love that always scoots over when children arrive with wide eyes and bad dreams. And I whisper it for all of us: "Deliver us from evil." Because who knew when we knelt down together in the snow on the campus of Notre Dame the night he asked me to marry him that we would live so much brave between then and now? I count years and bruises and late-night conversations in the desperate hours when children are finally asleep and we're almost too tired to remember what it is we're talking about. Some days we wonder if we'll make it. Nothing can hurt as much as the fears we carry for our children.

But we stand guard around their hearts and link arms around their stories and pray courage into the dark and the daylight and the school decisions and the friends who will influence them, stretch them, and mark them with their own choices, and we keep showing up. At the dinner table, at soccer matches, at baseball practices, at parent-teacher conferences, and at their bedsides. We show up and load the laundry and the words that need to be said again and again and again.

And while many mornings I'm tempted to hide away from being a grown-up, I can hear the shower running and I know Pete is awake and already facing the day for us. He'll see us through another one. When the bills are rising and the lions are roaring, he will carry us on his shoulders and make up the lilting nonsense songs that make us laugh as he fights a way safely home for us.

I don't know who these children will grow up to be. But I know that they have grown me up and dragged me out of myself. I have the scars to prove it. Peter told me once that God gave him a choice. What feels like several lifetimes ago, God gave him a choice to stay or to walk away from the girl who was rambling on, homesick about her broken heart buried alongside her mother in the red South African dirt.

We were both just twenty-one, baby grown-ups, and walking the fine line of throwing our everything in together, when I laid out all my baggage on the bare floor of that tiny apartment in downtown DC that I shared with two girlfriends. God told him that it would be okay to walk away. But that if he chose to stay, it would be a forever choice. A choice that meant he'd be the one to give and give and give until this girl was full up and healed in all her aching, broken places. A love gift, he gave me himself, his presence, his patience, and now his children. He trusted them to the woman who wasn't sure she'd ever be ready to want them. I needed a place to hide away, and he opened his arms and his life. He stayed.

Like my mother, I married a Peter, and he has been my rock.

• • •

On Friday nights we all stay in. We have pizza and a movie and three kids scrunched onto a single couch cushion because this is how they like it. Except for whoever ends up in the middle. We are a family that never gets tired of a good story. By Friday night, I don't care what state the laundry is in, and everyone eats off paper plates. I care about slowing down, doing less, being present more. Zoe doesn't care what we're watching—only that she's as close to her brothers as she can get. Micah has strong feelings about the kind of sauce and cheese and brand of pizza. Jackson will eat just about any slice you hand him. Pete and I settle in alongside them and sometimes watch computer screens instead because we can't take another round of *Kung Fu Panda*.

But many nights we just watch them—this crew of ours. We watch how much Micah looks like my brother Luke and catch each other's eyes over their heads and grin at something we know Luke would have said just exactly like that.

We try not to laugh as we listen to Jackson wax philosophical at some ordinary question Micah has asked or shake and shimmy his tiny heinie in perfect imitation of how my brother Josh would do it. And we make sure to keep our arms open, because Zoe will get bored of the movie and toddle over to check in and get a bear hug from time to time.

Someone will inevitably place a slice of pizza sauce down on the ottoman, and I will shriek and sigh, and a reluctant chorus of "Sorry, Mom" will rise from the faces that aren't looking my way at all. At some point they'll get tired of the movie and troop out to the backyard to see if their favorite neighbor kid, Eric, is around. They might hang on the fence and yell in the direction of his house even though we've told them a hundred times not to.

And if Eric comes out, there will be epic battles of the imagination and complex roles and weaponry and shrieks and fights and making up and starting over as Zoe wobbles her way between them all on Muppet-like legs, totally at home in this band of brothers.

I've long since given up trying to tame the backyard. The most we hope for is that all the toys are returned to the big galvanized plastic tub before everyone turns in for the night. But the apocalypse of holes dug by eager builders or military officers or pirate captains? Those I've made my peace with, and when I catch my reflection through the sliding-glass door as I stand surveying my kids at home in this landscape of their creation, I raise an eyebrow at myself and mutter,

"Hard to believe, isn't it?" The glory of motherhood camouflaged in so much chaos.

Later at night, when I want to soak in the bathtub, it will be full of a riot of toys, and there will be two pairs of muddy jeans, underpants, sneakers, and the worst-smelling socks in the world discarded alongside it no matter how many times I've pointed like a lunatic at the laundry basket. I will hear boys laughing between bunk beds, and I won't have the heart to yell about it and instead will walk down the hallway to check on the baby girl who wants her brothers to come and say good night. And they will. They always stop what they're doing to clump down the hall to her bedroom and dangle themselves over the edge of her crib to kiss her expectant face. She accepts this as her birthright.

Pete will navigate the boys' toothbrushes and bright-blue toothpaste that leaves trails all over the sink, and we'll try not to snap when what should be a simple routine derails into a spitting contest. Somehow they eventually end up in their beds. Until we open their favorite Bible storybook, and the one on the top bunk has to come down for a better look and the one on the bottom bunk has to rearrange himself closer to the pictures, and I have to take a deep swig of oxygen and remind myself that one day, theoretically, I'll miss this. And after we've read and someone has prayed and I've reminded someone else that a list of all the things you think your friends have done wrong isn't quite what I had in mind when asking for prayer requests, it suddenly occurs to them that they're exhausted. One barely has the will or the strength to make it back up the bunk bed ladder, and the other can hardly find the strength to pull up his duvet. I hold on to my temper with both hands, and we make it through.

But as I'm turning out the light and ready to turn the corner, sometimes one of them says, "Tell me about you and Dad again, Mom," and they know they've got me. Two blond heads with summer buzz cuts turn expectantly on their pillows as I pause in the door frame, outlined by the light. This is their favorite story. Because they know it's my favorite too.

Pete is already settled in on the sofa, and I'm so close to being there with him, so close to curling up with the yellow blanket, a generous helping of chocolate, and my own movie night. But someone has propped his chin on his hand and someone else has a slow grin growing, so I lean toward them and whisper, "Let me tell you the one about how I didn't think I wanted to be a mom." And they squeal and sit up in bed with happy sighs and eager faces, because they already know from the inside out and all the way down to their belly buttons how that story ends.

The glory of
motherhood comes
camouflaged in so
much chaos.

a letter to my mother

DEAR MOM,

You were only forty-two when you died. I am thirty-eight and painfully aware for the first time how young you were. Young enough to love Bruce Springsteen and dancing with Dad in the living room or out on the driveway as you waved us off to school. It's frozen in my memory. The outline of you in your light-blue sleep shirt dancing barefoot in our driveway as Dad pulled out of the garage and into the street. You would wave and dance us good-bye almost every morning that I remember. Dad called you Jo-babe, and you were a wild mix of who I have grown up into.

You'd send us out by bike late at night to pick up a Coke and a slab of chocolate for you when you were working into the wee hours. Firstborn. Gypsy yourself. You were a mother to kids born in three different countries. Lover of books and stories, you had me at the same age I got married. I still have all your books, and they've been good friends to me in my homesick years. How you loved languages! You spoke

German, Dutch, English, and Afrikaans, and you taught Latin. I got the best parts of my mothering from you—and also the worst.

How I find my comfort in books and familiar words because of you. How you would lock yourself in the bedroom and refuse to drive me to drama practice and insist I had to take my bike instead because you were stuck near the ending of a good book. Jackson has inherited the same gene—the love for losing yourself in a story.

Oh Mom, I've missed you.

Lately I've missed you more. I've cracked open a door to remembering what life looked like with you in it, and all kinds of strong feelings have blown in along with the memories. I parent deliberately these days. Less fly-by-the-seat-of-my-pants, more thought. You would love my sons. Jackson wears your name and your love for story so close to his skin, I'm amazed to watch how DNA can move through the generations. He eats movies, and imaginary characters loom so large in his mind that I know we will have to guard what he consumes. Today he was looking for something to eat and informed me all he wanted was some junk food. It would make you laugh how passionate he is about chocolate.

Micah challenges me. People tell me he looks like Luke, and I see it—all Dutch-born genes looming out of his blue eyes and fair skin. He is built for rugby, but if he grows up stateside, I'd say football is in his future. Some days the juxtaposition of his temper and bulk with his sensitive spirit can make it hard for him to navigate his world. He pours so much love into his puppy that I know the rightness of agreeing to add a dog to our circle of crazy despite what it costs me in irritation.

I want you to meet Zoe, Mom. She has unmade me and then put me back together again. And this time the parts of me that got broken after you died seem to have jigsawed themselves into place. I can see the whole picture, and I am surprised how beautiful it is. She takes my hand, and her chubby fingers fold my soul into her palm.

Zoe is teaching me how you loved me. That you loved me much deeper and longer than I could possibly remember. That you loved me at midnight and for three years in Zululand and during our stint stateside and even in standard six, when my skin broke out and you tried to take me for that facial.

Everything I can't remember about you I see reflected in Zoe's eyes. I am terrified by how much I love her. How did you bear the good-bye? Twenty years. *Twenty years.* It hurts to type it. Twenty years ago I sat in a pew and sang the last words you left for us:

Whatever my lot, Thou hast taught me to say,
"It is well, it is well, with my soul."

One week after I'd turned eighteen. I'm thirty-eight today. And I'm still singing it, Mom. I'm singing it still, and I still believe every hard, awful word to be true. That we can sing though the heavens crash open and the world comes pouring down around us. We can raise our eyes and our voices to the hills, where our help comes from, and sing. Even when all that comes out is a whisper.

> *Whatever my lot, Thou hast taught me to say,*
> *"It is well, it is well, with my soul."*

I bought knee-high boots last year—the first pair since the ones I owned when I was eighteen. I think you'd like them. They're a burnt umber kind of suede, and they make me feel brave.

Like riding bareback in the karoo.

Like walking the ridge of Table Mountain.

Like taking the train from Ukraine to Hungary.

Like changing my first diaper.

I am growing into brave, and I have two sons and a daughter, just like you did. We would light your smile on fire. All the frenetic life in this small house, all the clamoring to be loved. It makes crying okay. Because you can be sad and you can be well at the same time. Kingdom kids, Mom. I'm working hard to raise Kingdom kids with eyes for more than themselves. Past Jackson's tae kwon do and Micah's soccer, past what I haven't decided to make for dinner yet, past Zoe's looming terrible twos, and past the last of the needles from the Christmas tree that are still buried in the carpet months after the tree got thrown out. We're looking and listening past it all, holding on to your second chance with both hands.

And we are so well.

acknowledgments

To Peter. You have been my best friend ever since I passed that note all the way across class to you when I should have been paying attention. I love that we've written three children together. You make Mondays less scary. Thank you for facing all those lions for us. And for always loving me at my most unlovely. You are my rock. And I stand by what I promised you fifteen years ago when we exchanged wedding rings: "Where you go, I will go."

To Jackson, Micah, and Zoe. Look in my eyes. Listen carefully: "I love you. I love you. I love you." You are the best part of every day. Even the tired days. Even the days when we are all crabby. You are always the best part. Keep coming into bed every morning, and I'll keep sharing my pillow. You three are my favorite.

To Peter and Wanda Rous, for teaching me that home is a person and not just a time zone and that Jesus is the bridge who lays Himself down, plank by plank, to connect us, no matter how great the distance. Thank you for showing me what it looks like to throw your everything in to follow Him. And that sometimes the best sermons look like opening your front door to kids and more kids. Ek is so dankbaar.

To my South African family, thank you for loving me despite the onset of an American accent. For always welcoming me home without missing a beat, for coming out in full force to the airport whether we're arriving or departing, and for remembering the nooks and crannies of my mom—the good, the desperately sad, and the incredibly redeemed. Especially to my brothers, Joshua and Luke, because we bear the same scars and the same Savior, and I'm so thankful that I got to hold your hands on this journey of hurt and healing and growing up together.

To Lee and Debbie Baker, for your years of unconditional generosity and tireless prayers through the dark valleys and the beautiful sunrises. You have modeled what we can only hope to return. Thank you for being my roots in America. But mostly, thank you for Peter.

To my American family, for how you threw open your lives and your arms and drew this South African girl into your every days and holidays and celebrations and homes and rhythms and never once made me feel like an outsider. You are the reason I have felt so deeply, satisfyingly at home in the States from the beginning. Go Tigers!

To the women who read my blog and bleed their stories and failures and mothering victories into my comment box. This sisterhood that gets what it's like to live your own wants out of life in the leftovers of the day. Where would we be without one another to hold up the tired arms, to rub the knotted shoulders, to help fold the laundry? You are my people.

To Tara Phillips, for loving on our kids so faithfully and so creatively while I wrote these words. For seeing the backstage version of our family and still showing up the next day with a sense of humor and joy intact. And thank you for always, always unloading the dishwasher! You are family to us.

To Ann Voskamp, my word sister and soul sister and mentor and cheerleader and the wisest "farm hick" I know. Thank you for loving this little sister just the way I am and being the most faithful Jonathan to me and this fourth baby. My sofa is always your sofa.

To Lisa Milman, for living real life alongside me. In my messy playroom and chaotic car and late-to-school pickups. Thank you for seeing me in my everyday ins and outs and taking me anyway. And a thousand thanks for all the glorious hand-me-downs for Zoe.

To Jonathan and Christie Purifoy, for opening your home to me and my laptop for three of the most sacred days of writing. The final two chapters are a gift straight from Maplehurst, and I will always be grateful. I love that you've lived the story with us ever since the beginning, before any of us had (or wanted) kids.

To Bob and Colleen Skinner and Cliff and Heike Wright, for being a home away from home in Ukraine and a living exclamation point for what Christ is doing through His missionaries.

To Holley Gerth, for believing and cheering and enabling the dream growing in me before I even properly recognized it myself. Thank you for being the person on the other side of that first, wistful e-mail.

To Hilary Sherratt. I think Jesus introduced me to you so I could see what a wonder a grown-up daughter is. Thank you for filling me with anticipation. I can't wait to watch you write your own family.

To Kristen Strong, for holding the first drafts of this book in your hand and always sharing what you loved about it and why. You helped make me brave.

To Annie Downs, for walking this road with me through text messages and reassuring me that it was okay to cry in Panera while writing.

To Jennifer Dukes Lee, for your generous friendship and tireless example of a life lived where the Kingdom is always first and foremost a co-op and not a competition.

To Bill Jensen, agent, teacher, and reminder of the fun in publishing and the joy in storytelling.

To the Tyndale House team, for holding this story so tenderly and with such enthusiasm. Special thanks to Lisa Jackson, for seeing a story in me long before I did. To Eric Siewert, for being the first person to make me believe others might actually want to read this book. To Stephanie Rische, for her patient and gentle editor's touch. To Maria Eriksen, for her passionate promotion of this book. And to Kara Leonino, for faithfully praying every Thursday.

To the DaySpring (in)courage team—the most generous, inspired, creative, encouraging, and remarkable group I have ever been a part of. With special mentions to Saul Robles: you inspire me with what you have taught about hospitality and generosity. Thank you for being a tireless encourager and a man of such sincere integrity and delightful good humor. Mandy Butler, I love watching you love being a mama. And I've cherished our daily chats—such close colleagues from such a distance apart. Sally Haukas, you have a gentle Christ-wisdom way beyond your years. Thank you for always being willing to pray. Stephen Bos, thank you for encouraging and supporting our creativity and a love for Nando's chicken. And Jesse Lane, you will always be a part of this team to me. Thank you for never being afraid of big dreams.

To my Tuesday night girls from Calvary Church, thank you for doing real life alongside me. Thank you for sharing the messy stories and the stuck moments and the late nights and the Panera pastries.

To my (in)courage sisters, for walking and laughing and cheering and crying the journey together. For sharing links to bathing suits that flatter a mama's hips and the sense of humor in a story about poison ivy. For making community a safe place and writing our everyday stories a real and high calling.

To my Five Minute Friday community—the fearless writers who gather every Friday at my blog to just write without worrying if they get it just right or not. One writing prompt, just five minutes—you remind me all over again every week what it looks like to write brave. #FMFParty.

To Christa Wells and Nicole Witt, for your song "Pray," which became the soundtrack to the last chapter in this book and the anthem I will always hear in my head when I think of the story Jesus has written with my life.

And now to my Savior and Lord, Jesus Christ, "who is able to do immeasurably more than all we ask or imagine, according to his power that is at work within us, to him be glory in the church and in Christ Jesus throughout all generations, for ever and ever! Amen."[1]

notes

CHAPTER 4: A GREAT, BIG MAN NAMED CHUCK
1. 1 John 4:10, NLT (emphasis added)
2. 1 John 4:19, NLT

CHAPTER 5: TWO FUNERALS AND A BABY SHOWER
1. Horatio G. Spafford, "It Is Well with My Soul," 1873.

CHAPTER 9: THERE'S NOTHING ROUTINE ABOUT THE ROUTINE
1. Colossians 1:17 (emphasis added)

ACKNOWLEDGMENTS
1. Ephesians 3:20-21

glossary of
south african words

bakkie: Pickup truck. In South Africa, it's commonplace for kids, grown-ups, animals, and just about anything else to all ride together in the back of the pickup.

biltong: Dried, salted meat—usually of wild game. A sort of beef jerky equivalent, but much, much better. (My apologies, America, but it's true.)

bonnet: The British/South African term that refers to the car's hood, as we say in the States.

dassie: A hardy rabbit that lives in the rocky outcroppings in the South African veld.

karoo: A semidesert natural region of South Africa. Home to sheep farming and all my favorite childhood vacation memories.

koeksisters: A twisted braid of pastry that is deep fried and then dipped in sweet, sticky cold syrup. Served at all birthday parties, teas, church events, and school functions. Absolutely irresistible.

koppie: Small hill.

kraal: Fenced-in animal pen.

kuier: To visit for long, companionably protracted periods of time.

Marmite: Inherited from the British, this breakfast spread is black, has a very salty taste, and is a staple of all South African homes. Great on toast or crackers, especially when coupled with grated cheese and a slice of tomato, it's an acquired taste that you either love or hate.

mealie: Corn.

melktert: A pie with a filling the consistency of custard and topped with a dusting of cinnamon. Delicious. Served at absolutely all functions, gatherings, birthday parties, and teas. The one food my American husband asks for every year for his birthday.

netball: Like basketball, except not. Played only by women in two teams of seven each. Players must pass the ball down the court to score in the basket. A player can hold on to the ball for only three seconds when it's in her possession and must keep one foot on the spot she landed when she caught the ball. Players have specific positions that restrict where they can move on the court. Shots are scored through a hoop similar to a basketball hoop but much lower and without a backboard. Also, there is no dunking in netball. This was my favorite sport to play all through school, and it never once struck me as odd until I tried to explain it to my puzzled, grinning American husband one day when we were visiting home and I was standing in the center of the court I'd played on as a kid.

Nik Naks: Similar to American Cheetos. But for those of us raised on Nik Naks, there and there alone will our loyalty always lie.

ouma: Grandma.

oupa: Grandpa.

pap: Also known as mieliepap, this is a traditional porridge or polenta made from ground maize. It's a staple of many traditional South African dishes. It can be made different ways, but the most common kind—and the dish we always request when we're home—has a consistency so thick it can be held in the hand (called stywe pap).

Polyfilla: A spackling paste used to fill in holes or cracks in walls.

Provita crackers: A dry, bland brand of crackers that were the chosen snack of my childhood and many a church tea because of the creative ways you can dress them up. Marmite and grated cheese, jam and cheese, butter and apricot spread—you name it, the delicious options are endless.

rusk: A hard, biscotti-like baked good eaten with a cup of hot tea. Dip it into the tea to soften it, and then eat and enjoy.

sangoma: A Zulu word for a traditional healer or witch doctor.

sjambok: A whip fashioned out of leather strips traditionally made of adult hippopotamus or rhinoceros hide, although during apartheid, riot police were equipped with sjamboks made from plastic.

stywe pap: Stiff pap made from thick, white maize meal that is scooped into balls by hungry hands and dipped into the communal supper pot as a delicious pseudospoon.

veld: Tall, dry grass the color of wheat.

vetkoek: Über-tasty Afrikaans treat literally translated "fat cake." Gobs of dough are rolled into balls and then deep fried and served in either a savory (stuffed with minced meat/ground beef) or a sweet (sprinkled with powdered sugar or drizzled with honey or syrup) rendition. Lives up to its name in all the best ways.

vlakte: Vast, open plains or prairies.

about the author

LISA-JO BAKER and her husband have three kids who color their lives, complicate their frequent travel, and are the reason she believes motherhood should come with a superhero cape. A child of South Africa, Lisa-Jo grew up on karoo dust, purple jacaranda trees, and the stories of Zululand. While she came to the States for college and a law degree, she stayed for the boy from Michigan who became her husband.

They make their home under the cherry blossoms just outside Washington, DC, returning to the Southern Hemisphere whenever the craving for biltong and family gets too bad. Lisa-Jo is the social media manager for DaySpring, the Christian subsidiary of Hallmark, and the community manager for their website www.incourage.me. Lisa-Jo has blogged for Compassion International from Guatemala, is a contributor to HuffPost Parents, has been syndicated from New York to New Zealand, and shares her everyday life lived in between countries and kids at LisaJoBaker.com. She welcomes you to connect with her.

Twitter: @lisajobaker
Facebook: www.facebook.com/lisajobaker
Blog: www.lisajobaker.com

Hey there,

You read my book!

You now know more about me than I ever could have imagined sharing with a stranger. So we must be friends.

Friends with a story in common.

And I'd like to invite you deeper into the story.

Join me and my family as we partner with the nonprofit organization Take Action, in South Africa, to change the stories of hundreds of kids without mothers and hundreds of mothers who are mothering more kids than just their own.

So far, through Take Action, moms the world over have partnered together to build a water point, a laundry facility, and a vegetable garden, and they are working on a community center for a group of mothers, orphans, and vulnerable children just north of Pretoria, South Africa, in an area called Maubane.

Whether you are a mother, know a mother, or have a mother, come and Take Action with us.

Because there is nothing ordinary about being a mom, especially for the hundreds of kids who don't have one.

Join the movement at www.surprisedbymotherhood.com.

Lisa-Jo

CP0739

Try these other titles from Tyndale House Publishers: